Copyright © 2016 by Lani Sharp
All rights reserved. This book or any portion thereof
may not be reproduced or used in any manner whatsoever
without the express written permission of the publisher
except for the use of brief quotations in a book review.

Printed in Australia

First Printing, 2016

ISBN: 978-0-9925202-9-8

White Light Publishing House
6 Lincoln Way
Melton West, VIC, Australia 3337

www.whitelightpublishingau.com

❧ DEDICATIONS ☙

This book is dedicated to my partner Travis, the most inspiring Gemini in my Universe. Thank you for your love, faith, big heart, being such a wonderful part of my journey and father of our beautiful daughter - and of course for believing in my pipe dreams almost as much as I do. If we can survive Category 5 Cyclone Yasi (which also coincided with my birthday), we can surely survive anything. You had me at the amethyst necklace you gave me that very day, knowing it was my birthstone. Thank you for everything.

ABOUT THE AUTHOR

☾ ★ ☽

Lani Sharp is a Natural Born Rebel who just also happens to be an Aquarian, who shunned 'conventional' astrology courses to pursue her own path in the wondrous, inspiring and ever-evolving field of cosmic forces and stellar influences. After failing to find a course or tutor that suited her needs, Lani set out on her own starry Magic Carpet adventure across the skies, partly to discover her own 'truths' about this ancient system, but mostly to prove that one can achieve absolutely anything, including and above all, their dream careers (or lifestyle), if they put their hearts and souls into it. A self-taught astrologer who takes the esoteric and spiritual approach to this much-loved popular art, she has been studying and effectively practising astrology since she was eight years old. When she is not writing about, channelling, practising or teaching astrology, she can be found living her dream life alternating somewhere between her home in Australia's stunning Tropical North or her second home in Victoria's beautiful Dandenong Ranges, enjoying tea parties with her highly imaginative Cancerian daughter, Allira, and their gnome and fairy friends, crystal-wishing, day-dreaming, believing in gnomes, pixies, angels, fairies, magic and miracles, honing her magickal * witchcraft skills, Moon-gazing, Sun-worshipping, Venus-channelling, Jupiter-drawing, assisting others to discover, unravel and follow their true spiritual paths … or of course walking across rainbows!

* Not a mistake. Magick is a Wiccan variation of the word 'magic'.

ACKNOWLEDGEMENTS, CREDITS & GRATITUDE BLESSINGS

I would love to thank the following people and entities for their amazing contributions, interest, support and faith in me as I wrote the manuscripts for each of the twelve astrological Sun signs. Firstly, the biggest thank yous go to my Mum, Sandra, and my stepdad, Barry, for their unending support, love, advice, daily Skype conversations, acceptance of our geographical distance, and above all, their inner knowing that everything always comes together in the end. Your support of me and my dreams is appreciated beyond words.

Secondly, gratitude to my wonderful partner, Travis, for his patience (no mean feat for a Gemini!), for supporting me every step of the way, and for his acceptance of my 'mad scientist' Aquarian mindset by never trying to break down the invisible 'laboratory' walls I built around myself while writing the books. I would also like to extend my enormous gratitude to the following: Allira, my little Cancerian 'crab' daughter, a soul in a billion, who also had to tolerate and operate within the bounds of her nutty professor mother's antics and focus throughout the writing of the books. Thank you to Nicola, my wonderful Facebook friend, for recommending White Light Publishing House, and of course to White Light Publishing House themselves, for pouring their faith and passion into my project from the very beginning - and an even bigger thank you to the wonderful people behind the company for publishing my work, Christie and Jess! Gratitude also goes out to my dear friends, both near and far, who have inspired in me so many ideas through simply being themselves - especially Amanda and Carlie. Amanda, you have always been my 'astrology buddy' and I have always enjoyed - and learned so much through - our discussions on all things astrology and star signs: the good, the bad and the ugly! Having someone like you off which to bounce thoughts and share ideas with, has always been immensely helpful and appreciated.

I have saved my final thank you for The Universe, who always delivers to me exactly what I have asked for, without exception. The Universe is my ultimate *higher power*, my guiding light, my powerful driving force, my spiritual helper, my guardian angel, my eternal friend, my inner motivator, my sympathetic listener, my inspirational teacher, and the fulfiller of all my dreams, including this one, having my very first book(s) published, a long-held dream that stretches way back through the years to my days of being a mini dreamer, inquisitor and stargazer. The Universe has always believed in me, but perhaps more importantly, I have always believed in *IT*.

So to all of the above, I wish to say:

Thank you, thank you, thank you!

.

"There was a star danced,
and under that I was born"

William Shakespeare

"We were born at a given moment, in a given place, and like vintage years of wine, we have the qualities of the year and of the season in which we are born"

Carl G. Jung

INSPIRED BY ALL THE SIGNS

Aries imparted courage and boldness
And helped me dance away the pain
Taurus gave me hugs and comfort
And shelter from the rain
Gemini provided me with laughter
And taught me again how to have fun
Cancer nurtured and sustained me
By reflecting back my Sun
Leo reminded me there was joy
From within myself and above
Virgo awakened my healthy glow
By teaching me how to love
Libra gave me gentle hugs
And judged me not for a thing
Scorpio lent me some of his power
And took away the sting
Sagittarius showered me with gifts
Of words so wise and true
As Capricorn led the way up the mountain
My resolve and strength grew
Aquarius gave me the gift of friendship
And carried me as his brother
And Pisces swam with me to the depths
With a compassion like no other.

Special Note

Throughout the text of this book, and indeed the whole Lucky Astrology book series, I have capitalised the first letter of the word 'Universe'. This is because, quite simply, I feel it is a very special title for the higher power that I personally choose to be guided by, and have accordingly highlighted it as such.

You may also notice that I use the words 'he' or 'she', and 'his' or 'her', when referring to your own Sun sign and other zodiac signs, and never 'he or she' or 'his or her' together. The reason for this is for simplicity, for I don't wish the sentences to be too wordy and therefore the messages within them to be lost. As a general rule, I refer to all six 'masculine' zodiac signs as 'he', and all six 'feminine' signs as 'she', and this remains a consistent rule throughout this book and the whole series.

Your Sun sign, Gemini, is a masculine sign and will thus be referred to accordingly.

CONTENTS

	Page
ASTROLOGY	15
THE SUN	25
GEMINI THE TWINS	31
QUOTES BY GEMINIANS	38
THE GEMINI CONSTELLATION	42
THE GEMINI SYMBOL	45
THE RUNDOWN & LESSONS ★	
THE ESSENCE OF GEMINI	48
THE THREE DECANS OF GEMINI	59
YOUR ELEMENT ★ AIR	63
YOUR MODE ★ MUTABLE	86
YOUR RULING PLANET ★ MERCURY	89
YOUR HOUSE IN THE HOROSCOPE ★	
THE THIRD HOUSE	106
YOUR OPPOSITE SIGN ★ SAGITTARIUS	110
MAGIC, DRAWING, ATTRACTION, SPELLS,	
RITUALS, WISHING & POWER	120
ASTROLOGY & MAGIC	125
PLANETS ★ DAYS OF THE WEEK	
& THEIR POWERS	131
YOUR NATAL MOON PHASE	135
SPELLS, MAGIC & WISHING WITH MOON PHASES	138
THE MOON ★ WHAT IT REPRESENTS IN THE HUMAN	
PSYCHE & NATAL CHART	145
YOUR MOON SIGN	148
YOUR BODY & HEALTH	156
THE CELL SALTS ★ ASTROLOGICAL TONICS	161

	Page
AIR SIGN GEMINI & THE SANGUINE HUMOUR	164
MONEY ATTRIBUTES	167
COLOURS ★ YOUR LUCKY COLOURS	170
LUCKY CAREER TIPS	181
LUCKY PLACES	186
GEMS & CRYSTALS	187
GEMINIAN POWER CRYSTALS	201
YOUR LUCKY NUMBERS	208
YOUR LUCKY MAGIC HOURS OR TIME UNITS	217
YOUR LUCKY DAY ★ WEDNESDAY	222
YOUR LUCKY CHARM / TALISMANS	226
YOUR LUCKY ANIMALS & BIRDS	229
YOUR METALS	241
PLANTS, HERBS, SPICES, TREES, SHRUBS, FLOWERS, SCENTS & INCENSE	245
YOUR SPECIAL POWER FLOWERS	249
YOUR FOODS	251
YOUR LUCKY WOOD & CELTIC TREE ★ ELDER, FILBERT, BEECH & HAWTHORN OR OAK	254
THE POWER OF LOVE	263
LUCKY IN LOVE? GEMINI COMPATIBILITY	276
YOUR TAROT CARDS ★ THE LOVERS, THE MAGICIAN & THE FOOL	294
LUCKY 13 TIPS	315
HAVE YOU PACKED YOUR MAGICAL BAG FOR THE JOURNEY?	318
A FINAL WORD ★ TAPPING INTO THE MAGIC OF GEMINI	319

LUCKY ASTROLOGY

By Lani Sharp

GEMINI

Tapping into the Powers of Your Sun Sign for Greater Luck, Happiness, Health, Abundance & Love

"That which is above is like to that which is below, and that which is below is like to that which is above, to accomplish the miracles of one thing ... the Father thereof is the Sun, the mother the Moon."

The Emerald Tablet, Hermes Trismegistus (circa 3000 BC)

★ ASTROLOGY ★

Astrology: "Divination through the correlation
of earthly events with celestial patterns"
'Real Magic', I. Bonewits, 1971

A BRIEF HISTORY

Astrology can be defined as the calculation and meaningful interpretation of the positions and motions of the heavenly bodies, and their correlation with human experiences. Its central concept is based upon this interconnectedness or correspondence between the stars and ourselves.

The word astrology is derived from the Greek word astron, meaning 'star' and logos which means 'word'. Astrology, therefore, literally means language of the stars. It is based on the ancient law known as 'As Above, So Below', otherwise known as the Law of the Macrocosm and Microcosm. The Macrocosm is the Universe, symbolised by the sky, the starry dome that we can see from the Earth; the Microcosm is us - humans, and all other life on Earth. 'As Above, So Below' is a well-known and deeply impressing maxim of Hermetic origin, inscribed upon the famed Emerald Tablet among cryptic wording by enigmatic figure, Hermes Trismegistus, around 5,000 years ago. These four powerful words are adopted by astrologers and believers in magic to explain, in very succinct wording, the meaning behind the art and science of celestial influences upon our Earthly affairs.

Astrology and many other magical and occult studies, propose that we are not separate from the Universe, we are part of it. The Sun, Moon and planets all follow exact patterns of movement and their motions can be measured precisely by astronomers. The basic idea of astrology is that all individual parts of the Universe, from plants to animals, cooperate with each other and work together in harmony.

Anyone can apply astrological knowledge in their daily lives, but it hasn't always been like that. At one time, astrology was reserved only for Kings and nations, and only the court astrologer/astronomer could cast and interpret horoscopes. Ancient astrology and astronomy used to be one and the same. To be an astrologer, you first had to be able to interpret the stars in some systematic way, and then track the movement of the Moon and the planets against the background of the constellations.

Astrology, the knowledge and language of the cosmos, goes back to the ancient kingdom of Babylonia and was adapted by the Mesopotamians, Greeks, Egyptians and Romans to incorporate their own deities (as indicated in mythology). It is upon a combination of Greek and Egyptian interpretations of astrology that our present knowledge is based.

In the ancient Mesopotamian world, as far back as 800 BC, people lived precariously beneath the open skies. The skies and the stars which filled them, were the real founders of astrology. Today we are aware that the Sun and Moon exert a profound influence upon our Earthly affairs, but for our primitive ancestors, the heavens, the stars and the planets must have been a matter of great and mysterious significance. Early humankind, its senses influenced by natural processes of ebbs, flows, growth, decay and cycles, tended naturally towards a physical explanation of the Universe. At first, the movements of the planets - and all celestial occurrences - were observed as omens affecting the Ruler and his nation; it was only in Egypt in the fifth century AD that the casting of horoscopes for individual people and the calculation of the planetary positions at the time of birth became widespread.

The first astrologers, the Chaldeans, mapped the stars and later passed this knowledge and wisdom on to the ancient Greeks, who, during the third century BC, developed astrology into a science with the use of mathematical aids and instruments to measure planetary movements. The Greeks were the first to cast individual horoscopes. And it was the Greeks who associated the four elements with the signs of the zodiac. The word "zodiac" can be translated from Greek to mean the "circle or path of the animals." The Greeks not only had names for the twelve Solar phases but had symbols for each, and many correspond with the ones we use today.

The Greeks passed on much of their knowledge to the Romans. During the second century BC, Roman astrologers were primarily forecasters who were consulted frequently by rulers of the church and state. By the early third century AD, astrology co-existed with early Christianity. This harmonious co-existence was possible because it was considered that celestial bodies could foretell events, but did not determine the future - indeed, the stars seen by the shepherds at the time of Christ's birth were only predictors of his arrival. After the fourth century AD, Christianity strengthened and the popularity of astrology declined as Christian reluctance to support 'pagan' or 'superstitious' beliefs became more prominent. The Middle Ages saw a revival in astrology, with courses being taught in universities and other educational establishments, and connections were made between the zodiac, alchemy, herbs and medicine. Astrology was once again able to exist alongside the Church, although many remained suspicious of astrologers.

Around the beginning of the fifteenth century, academics of the Renaissance movement examined the past for knowledge, and ancient philosophies, including astrology, flourished; this coincided with arts and science movements developing. The famous prophet and astrologer Nostradamus lived during this period. Leonardo da Vinci depicted aspects of astrology combined with geometry in his art. Writers and poets of the time, including Shakespeare, alluded to zodiacal influences in their work.

During this period, astrology had numerous practical applications. Agricultural calendars were introduced, indicating favourable planting times according to the phases of the Moon; health and illness were linked with movements of celestial bodies; and emotional states and mental health afflictions correlated with the planetary positions.

Eventually, new ways of thinking led to a split between astronomy and astrology, and by the seventeenth century, the realm of science had developed to such a degree that astrology was no longer taken seriously.

The study of the sky above us has been charted for more than 5,000 years. This fact is known because ancient 'horoscopes' imprinted on clay tablets have been unearthed, dating back almost 5,400 years ago. However, no one knows for certain just how, when and where astrology first began, although it is known that it flourished in ancient Chaldea, Mesopotamia, Babylon and Egypt.

Astrology is a science which has spanned many centuries and still remains extraordinarily popular, and its truths have the potential to speak to and *through* all of us. Long before today's interest in it, men of great vision such as Ptolemy, Hippocrates, Plato, Galileo, Jefferson, Franklin, Newton, Columbus and Jung respected its inherent truths, mythology and eternal knowledge. Furthermore, astrology predates many other 'sciences' - for out of it grew religion, medicine and astronomy, not the other way around.

The discipline of astrology is ultimately a study of the interlocking and interrelated forces of the twelve zodiacal forces, or constellations, that grace the heavens, as they pour their energies into the Earthly kingdoms below. As these various energies circulate throughout the etheric realm of our Solar system, these zodiacal entities and archetypes imprint their vibrational frequencies and harmonic resonances upon our bodies, minds, souls and spirits.

ASTROLOGY & THE INDIVIDUAL

Since the earliest period of the history of humankind, people studied the starry vaults of the heavens and conceived that their presence, movements and positions endowed planet Earth's inhabitants with Divine influence. There is much evidence that positions and movements of the planets as seen from Earth at the time of a birth are linked to personality characteristics of individuals.

Human energy and emotional cycles are governed by the forces and networks of magnetic impulses from all the planets. Of all the heavenly bodies, the Moon's effects and power are the most marked and visible due to its close proximity to Earth. But the Sun, Venus, Mars, Mercury, Jupiter, Saturn, Uranus, Neptune and Pluto exercise their influences just as surely. In fact, scientists are aware that plants and animals are affected by natural cycles which are governed by forces such as fluctuations in barometric pressure, the gravitational field and electricity in the air. These Earthly dynamics are originally triggered by magnetic vibrations from the atmosphere, or outer space, from where the planets send forth their unseen waves. No living organism or mineral on Earth escapes these immense, if unseen, influences.

The geomagnetic field seems to affect life on Earth in certain observed ways, and these influences appear to correlate with planetary positions. It has been suggested that the fluctuations of the Earth's magnetic field are picked up by the nervous system of the in utero infant, which acts like an antenna, and these synchronise the internal biological clocks of the foetus which control the moment of birth. The foetal magnetic antenna therefore, is sensitive enough to sense these planetary vibrations and fields, and through a combination of inherited genetics and the positions of the planets at birth, they are imprinted with certain basic inherited and 'absorbed' personality characteristics.

Carl Jung, the Swiss psychiatrist and psychological theorist, suggested that the inherent disposition of the individual is present at birth, and is reflected in the patterns of his or her natal chart. Further, he theorised that there is a 'priori factor' in all human activities, namely the inborn, preconscious and unconscious individual structure of the psyche. The preconscious psyche, for example that of a newborn baby, is not simply an empty vessel into which practically anything can be poured, but rather it is this preconscious psyche that gives us the free will to become what we are instead of what others or our environment makes us. The child is not merely a receptacle for the psychic life of those around him or her, albeit sensitive and susceptible to the surrounding unconscious forces in childhood; for he/she also brings something of his own to his experience of them.

Further, Dr Harold S. Burr, who was a Professor of Anatomy at the Yale University School of Medicine, and author of *The Nature of Man and the Meaning of Existence* (1962), asserted that there is order in the Universe, unity in the organism and man is endowed with a soul. He stated that a complex magnetic field not only establishes the pattern of the human brain at birth, but continues to regulate and control it through life, and that the human central nervous system is a superb receptor of electro-magnetic energies, indeed the finest in nature. He contended that the electro-dynamic fields of all living things, which may be measured and mapped with standard voltmeters, mould and control each organism's development, health and mood, and named these fields 'fields of life'.

It can therefore be suggested that astrological and planetary influences endow us with the majority of our characteristics at birth, characteristics bestowed upon us according to our Sun sign and other planetary forces. Other parts of the chart are also highly significant and need to be integrated for a 'whole' picture to form, however the Sun sign is an excellent starting point.

The ancients taught that astrology was one of the keys to the many enigmas that plague humans in their unceasing quest to determine what the meaning of life is, and what their role and place in the Universe is - and this quest still persists today. Astrology, which dates back over 5,000 years, is indeed one such key to unlocking the many secrets of the Universe - and ultimately, the individual self.

"KNOW THYSELF"

"Man, know thyself.
All wisdom centres on this."
Carl Jung

Before the temple of the Oracle at Delphi, the ancient Greeks imparted a special piece of advice that was carved onto one of the portals: "Know Thyself." These two powerful words are easy enough to understand, but much more difficult to apply. Throughout life's inner and outer journey, astrology can provide us with an inner navigational system by which we can be guided towards our highest potential, and closer towards the eternal quest of 'knowing thyself'. It provides the hope that this higher spiritual plane exists and that if we can 'read' and therefore be guided by the unique inner blueprint that our individual birth chart has stamped upon us at the moment we take our very first breath, indeed we can reach this higher spiritual plane and realise our innate potential.

Always remember that astrology is not fatalistic. The stars may incline, but they do not compel. Astrology simply provides us with an inner guide, a blueprint, for our journey through life and the finding of our true selves - and what we do with the resulting knowledge is entirely up to us.

Good luck on your journey!

THE ZODIAC & YOUR PLACE IN THE SUN

The zodiac is a circle of 360 degrees, consisting of equal segments of 30 degrees each. These represent the twelve houses of the twelve astrological signs. This zodiac is how the early astrologers imagined the Solar system to be, a perfect circle with the Earth at its centre, around which the Sun, Moon and the planets revolved. Each sign of the zodiac corresponds to one of the twelve segments, following a chronological order and established according to the rhythm of the seasons and cycles of the Sun and the Moon. But the zodiac itself, or the band of constellations which comprise it, has shifted over the millennia, creating division between astronomical and astrological schools of thought. It has been said that due to this shift over time, one who once considered themselves as an Aquarian, is actually a Capricorn, the sign before it, and a Leo is actually a Cancerian, its preceding sign. This is the result of misunderstandings and differences in perspectives, and explanations around it are beyond the scope of this book, but can be researched further should you wish to delve a little deeper.

From the astronomical point of view, it is true that the zodiac to which we refer today is not situated where it 'should' be, but indeed, nothing is fixed under the celestial vault. And so the starting point of the ancient zodiac does not correspond exactly to the one we can observe today. But for the purposes of increasing your power and luck, let's keep things simple and enjoy the ride; after all, astrology - while based upon many scientific theories, mysteries, scepticism, superstitions, facts, measurable patterns, ambiguities, correlations, paradoxes, contradictions, links, stigmatisms and observations that seek to support, refute, prove and disprove this ancient art time and again - is ultimately meant to be *fun* too!

THE SUN

Earth's Luminary ★ *Our Brightest Shining Star*

Our Centre, Core Self, Identity & Inner Guiding Light

"Perfect is what I have said of the work of the Sun."
Hermes Trismegistus, The Emerald Tablet

The Sun is our essence, centre, source, ego strength, power, life force, will, vitality, creative expression, purpose, life's direction, our sense of identity, and who we really *are*. Our brightest star is the core of our individuality, our inner guiding light. The Sun is externalising, and represents totality, infinity, eternity, the striving toward and ultimate reaching of one's personal destiny, and *completion* in all areas. It is the creative energising giver of life and the 'father' of the zodiac. It endows us with our inherent creative potential and personal identity - our urge to *create* and to *be*. The Sun is our core self, conscious purpose, our sense of creating something out of our own being. It is the integrated personality and represents the *present*, our greatest Gift. The Sun rules the heart and is thus symbolically the centre of Self. Indeed, the Sun *is* the heart and the most commanding presence in our birth chart; the luminary Ruler who governs our essential self and wants to be noticed and appreciated, and above all, to *shine*.

★ KEY WORDS ★

Identity, core self, spirit, life force, power, essence, creativity, higher self, the Father, ego, vitality, pride, individuality, leadership, majesty, inner authority, will, expression, willpower, purpose, the journey, the path and the destiny.

THE SUN ★ THE ULTIMATE SOURCE OF LIFE ON EARTH

Throughout the ages, and indeed since life forms began, the electromagnetic waves generated by the Sun have kept planet Earth habitable for humans, animals, plants and minerals. The Sun is, in fact, the only true source of energy on planet Earth. It provides the perfect amount of energy for plants to synthesise all of the products required for growth and reproduction, which is then stored by plants and ingested by humans and animals who, through many complex processes, utilise these various forms of encapsulated Solar energy - and so the cycle continues. Wood, fuel and minerals (crystals included), too, are merely various forms of this encased Sun energy. In fact all matter is essentially 'frozen' light. Human body cells are bundles of Sun energy; we couldn't conceive or process a single thought without the molecules of Solar-energised oxygen and glucose.

In essence, the Sun supports the growth of all species, including human beings and microscopic life forms, and without it life on Earth would simply not be possible. The mathematical and metaphysical complexity that stands behind a system of organisation and order so infinitely diverse and intricate as planetary life cannot be truly fathomed, but unerringly and miraculously, the Sun instinctively knows what each species, from a tree to a human, intrinsically needs in order to fulfil its evolutionary purpose and cycles.

Ultimately, the electromagnetic waves generated by the Sun come in a variety of lengths, which determine their specific course of action and responsibility. There are gamma rays, x-rays, cosmic rays, various kinds of ultraviolet rays, infrared, short-wave infrared, radio waves, electric waves, and of course the visible light spectrum, consisting of the seven colour rays.

Most of these energy waves are absorbed and used for various processes in the layers of atmosphere that encircle the Earth, and only a small portion of them - the electromagnetic spectrum - reach the surface of our planet. Although the human eye is only able to perceive about one percent of this spectrum, the waves exert a very strong influence upon us. The waves and rays which do affect us so profoundly, allow all life forms to undergo constant cycles of change necessary for growth and renewal. Physically, we can observe this, but on a deeper, more spiritual plane, we can even *feel* it and allow its radiance to permeate our very souls. Such is the might, force and power of that astonishing ball of fire in our sky: the brilliant, ever-shining Sun.

THE SUN ★ WHAT IT REPRESENTS IN THE HUMAN PSYCHE & NATAL CHART

☼

"The Sun is the most powerful of all the stellar bodies. It colours the personality so strongly that an amazingly accurate picture can be given of the individual who was born when it was exercising its power through the known and predicable influences of a certain astrological sign; these electromagnetic vibrations will continue to stamp that person with the characteristics of their Sun sign as they go through life."
Linda Goodman's Sun Signs, Linda Goodman, Pan Books, 1968

The Sun is our essence, our core self, conscious purpose and sense of identity, our creative potential, our spirit, the integrated personality that shines outward from within us. It is concerned with the present. It is our centre, source, power, life force, will, vitality, purpose, life's direction, what and who we *really* are.

The Sun represents our basic urge for self-expression. It is the 'Solar energy cell' in a person's character, the Lord and giver of life, and symbolises the way in which an individual will shine out to the world. Our Sun is our personal identity and aspects to it from other components in the chart show the ease or otherwise of assuredness and confidence with which one will project and express one's individuality. The Sun sign will also show how an individual bounces back from setbacks and disappointments, their resilience and their general outward expression of energy.

The Sun is the archetype of the Father and represents the primary masculine principle in the natal chart. It indicates how we express and experience our masculine side, or animus, our conscious self, how we express ourselves creatively, our personal potential, individuality, self-expression and personal power. It has to do with courage, power, generosity, creativity, vitality, self-confidence, nobility, self-worth, dignity and strength of will. It symbolises authority and purpose, the *ruler*, and its potential is the peak of constructive maturity. It signifies self-sufficiency and abundance, containing enough energy to radiate warmth and give life to everything around it.

The sign in which one's Sun is posited, and its placement in the birth chart, strongly indicates the level and type of vitality available to the personality (the sign), and in which area of life this may be most strongly directed (the house).

The Sun in a natal chart is a powerful symbol because everything is filtered, at a conscious level, through it. It tells us what we need to do to feel fully alive, the type of engine 'driving' us, what we need to do to be authentic and to be fully functioning. Listening to the special message of one's Sun sign can provide one with greater direction, and a more dynamic energy and life purpose.

The symbol for the Sun ☉ depicts a circle with a dot or 'seed' at its centre, from which the core self, power, creativity and the first sparks of life can spring. The circle around this 'seed' represents spirit, symbolising wholeness, eternity and the never-ending flow of energy.

While the Moon, the night sky's luminary, represents the *soul*, the Sun, the day sky's luminary, represents our *spirit*.

There is a reason your Sun sign is otherwise known as your Star Sign - it's because, quite simply, the Sun *is* a star; in fact, it's the largest, brightest, shiniest one in Earth's known visible Universe. This book is about your Sun sign and how you can become much larger, glow with far more brilliance, and shine brighter than you ever dreamed possible. I wish you all the magic in the galaxy for your dreams to come true and your deepest wishes to become reality, through tapping into the amazing power and inherent potential of your Sun sign. So get set for a galactical ride through the lucky stars of your constellation - and may a shooting star cross the path in front of you as you go!

GEMINI THE TWINS

★ Mutable Air, Masculine, Positive, Thinking ★

"The mind communicates streams of information"

Body & Health
Hands, Shoulders, Arms, Lungs, Body Tubing, Nervous System

How Gemini Emanates its Life Force / Energy
Rapidly, skilfully, with versatility and wit

Is Concerned With
★ Communication, speech, articulation ★
★ Dexterity, nimbleness, light-footedness ★
★ Change, variety ★ Wit, persuasion ★
★ Knowledge ★ Freedom, youth ★ Agility ★
★ Movement ★ Curiosity ★ Short journeys ★
★ Education ★ Learning ★ Gathering facts ★
★ Adaptability ★ Intellect ★ The Mind ★

Spiritual Gemini

Your Archetypal Universal Qualities
The Communicator, Networker, Student

What You Refuse
To stay still or be pinned down

What you Are an Authority On
Mental and communicative abilities, fun

The Main Senses Through Which You Experience Your Reality
Thought, perception, speech, communication

How You Love
Youthfully, with charm

Positive Characteristics
★ Inquisitive ★ Interesting ★ Versatile ★ Clever ★ ★ Flirty ★ Fun ★ Engaging ★ Youthful ★ ★ Enchanting ★ ★ Quick ★ Witty ★ Agile ★
★ Liberal ★ Broad-minded ★ ★ Stimulating ★
★ Charming ★ Unprejudiced ★

Negative Characteristics
★ Restless, changeable, inconsistent ★
★ Superficial and shallow ★
★ Impatient and irritable ★ Nervous ★ Fickle ★
★ Dual personality ★
★ Impractical ★ Manipulative ★
★ Non-committal, flighty ★ Gossipy ★
★ Easily bored, short attention span ★ Capricious ★ ★ Cunning ★ Cheeky ★

To Bring Out Your Best
Travel to offbeat intellectually-awakening places, chat-rooms and other social exchanges on the

internet, attend parties, stay occupied and mentally stimulated, and undertake short courses.

Spiritual Goals
To learn how to explore things in greater depth; to endure and face things head on; to be more consistent and reliable by keeping promises; to fight rather than take flight, to learn the value of commitment and endurance; to set long-term goals.

GEMINI

21 May - 20 June

Mutable Air

♊

Ruled by Mercury

"I THINK"

Gemstones ◊ Alexandrite, Agate, Citrine

★ Adaptable, fickle, nervous, eloquent, scattered, superficial, versatile, talkative, cunning, busy, candid, curious, witty, youthful, inquisitive, lively, spontaneous, charming, inconstant, indecisive, fun, alert, intelligent, restless, friendly, flighty, open-minded, glib, insincere, dexterous, impatient, sociable, communicative, moral, inquiring, mischievous, clear, shifty, excitable, agile ★

"Imperfection is beauty, madness is genius, and it's better to be absolutely ridiculous than absolutely boring"
Marilyn Monroe

GEMINI

♊

★ Fun ★ Sociable ★ Curious ★ Superficial ★ Restless ★ Adaptable ★ Intelligent ★ Versatile

Gemini is the sign of the Twins, two childlike figures who represent the dual nature of this sign. Versatile, two-faced, sociable, childish, talkative, cunning, flirtatious, curious, superficial and inquisitive are Geminis' most notable traits. Being an intellectual air sign, this sign is the flightiest of the air signs, being mutable and therefore very changeable and easily bored by sameness and distracted and influenced by any interesting 'flavours of the month' presenting themselves.

Constantly on the move, restless and nervous, Geminis need to be occupied at all times. If they are not feeling stimulated by activity, this nervous energy can become destructive and they are prone to childish tantrums and selfish sulking, before quickly recovering and bounding jubilantly into their next adventure. The Twins are never mad for long, given their short attention span, flitting instead from one situation or interest to the next, with little reflection or brooding over past upsets.

Cunning and witty, the Twins are often the class clown and revel in the resulting attention. Charming in an innocent and almost childlike way, Gemini is the life of the party and is easily recognised as the one who is moving from person to person engaging in refreshing, albeit superficial, exchanges around the punch bowl. A fun and flirty lover, light-hearted friend and a clever jack-of-all-trades, Gemini is the third sign and the cheeky Peter Pan of the zodiac, never quite growing up but always managing to pull it off with a refreshingly breezy pizzazz!

KEY CONCEPTS

★ Cheeky and mischief-making ★
★ Light-hearted and cheerful ★
★ Restless, troublesome and easily bored ★
★ Refreshing lack of ego but plenty of dash ★
★ Alert, flexible and agile mind ★
★ Silly and inane ★
★ Charming, clever conman and trickster ★
★ Super-intellectual, all words and talk ★
★ Dissipates self through lack of focus ★
★ Unemotional and impatient with others' emotions ★
★ Nervous and excitable ★
★ Intelligent, versatile and adaptable ★
★ Clear, precise and objective insight and intellect ★

SOME CORRESPONDENCES THAT ARE ASSOCIATED WITH GEMINI

Books, duality, languages and linguistics, lungs, news, communication, taxis, libraries, reporters, the hands, alertness, short journeys, the mind, post offices, lectures, advertising, telephones, respiratory system, journalists, merchandising, railways, trains, accountants, publications, the arms, twins, schools and teachers, manicurists, the press, book shops, messengers, correspondence, restlessness, transporting, graphologists, intelligence agents, vehicles, nervous system, interviews, publishers, dexterity, commuting, writers, postal workers, documents, runners, manuscripts, secretaries, couriers, nerves, car dealers, clerks, visitors, translators, conversation, enquiries, information, roads, printers and quicksilver. Take your pick and enjoy the ride!

QUOTES BY GEMINIANS

"Whatever course you decide upon, there is always someone to tell you that you are wrong. There are always difficulties arising which tempt you to believe that your critics are right. To map out a course of action and follow it to an end requires courage" - Ralph Waldo Emerson (25 May 1803)

"What's missing from pop music is danger" - Prince (7 June 1958)

"Do not go where the path may lead, go instead where there is no path and leave a trail" - Ralph Waldo Emerson

"When written in Chinese, the word 'crisis' is composed of two characters - one represents danger and the other represents opportunity" - John F. Kennedy (29 May 1917)

"The only creatures that are evolved enough to convey pure love are dogs and infants" - Johnny Depp (9 June 1963)

"If slaughterhouses had glass walls, everyone would be a vegetarian" - Paul McCartney (18 June 1942)

"One great strong unselfish soul in every community could actually redeem the world" - Elbert Hubbard (19 June 1856)

"I've been reckless, but I'm not a rebel without a cause" - Angelina Jolie (4 June 1975)

"When we truly care for ourselves, it becomes possible to care far more profoundly about other people. The more alert and sensitive we are to our own needs, the more loving and generous we can be towards others" - Eda LeShan (6 June 1922)

"When kids hit one year old, it's like hanging out with a miniature drunk" - Johnny Depp

"Always be a first-rate version of yourself, instead of a second-rate version of somebody else" - Judy Garland (10 June 1922)

"Silence is argument carried out by other means" - Ernesto 'Che' Guevara (14 June 1928)

"If any of you cry at my funeral, I'll never speak to you again!" - Stan Laurel (16 June 1890)

"It was Elvis who really got me hooked on beat music. When I heard Heartbreak Hotel I thought, 'This is it'" - Paul McCartney

"I think everybody's nuts" - Johnny Depp

"Follow your inner moonlight; don't hide the madness" - Allen Ginsberg (3 June 1926)

"How strange when an illusion dies. It's as though you've lost a child" - Judy Garland

"Women won't let me stay single and I won't let me stay married" - Errol Flynn (20 June 1909)

"I tried being reasonable, I didn't like it" - Clint Eastwood (31 May 1930)

"Courage is being scared to death - and saddling up anyway" - John Wayne (26 May 1907)

"The truth is, I've never fooled anyone. I've let men sometimes fool themselves" - Marilyn Monroe (1 June 1926)

"You need a lot of luck to find people with whom you want to spend the rest of your life. Some people manage to find their soul mate. Others don't. I think love is like a lottery" - Kylie Minogue (28 May 1968)

"I have a very strict gun control policy: if there's a gun around, I want to be in control of it" - Clint Eastwood

"I wouldn't be caught dead marrying a woman old enough to be my wife" - Tony Curtis (3 June 1925)

"I'm sure that love exists, even infinite, eternal love" - Kylie Minogue

"That man's silence is wonderful to listen to" - Thomas Hardy (2 June 1840)

"All men can live together, if they wish to" - Josephine Baker (3 June 1906)

"Women who seek to be equal with men lack ambition" - Marilyn Monroe

"The answer, my friend, is blowin' in the wind, the answer is blowin' in the wind" - Bob Dylan (24 May 1941)

"I'm selfish, impatient and a little insecure. I make mistakes. I am out of control and at times hard to handle. But if you can't handle me at my worst, then you sure as hell don't deserve me at my best" - Marilyn Monroe

"In spite of everything, I still believe people are really good at heart" - Anne Frank (12 June 1929)

THE GEMINI CONSTELLATION

The signs of the zodiac are the twelve symbolic features that ancient people imagined while observing the heavens. They saw shapes, patterns, faces, and natural and supernatural beings in the stars, from which they established, over centuries, a kind of celestial hierarchy and system based upon their observations. Groupings of stars became constellations, and twelve of these constellations make up the zodiac, a Greek word meaning 'circle of animals', that we know today.

Star constellations are not really self-contained groups but are particularly bright stars that give the appearance of being close together and form distinctive patterns. These are the patterns that over the ages have been identified as animals, deities or mythological figures and heroes. The stars are the living past. We receive their light long after it has left the star itself and so they are a good focus for escaping from the parameters of time. Their stellar influence is analogous with the aura, the bio/psychic energy field surrounding humans, animals, plants, crystals and even places. These individual energy systems interact with the energy waves emanated by other people, and even the cosmic rays emitted by planetary bodies, for psychic energies are not limited by time or distance.

The cluster of stars we know as Gemini the Twins are Castor and Pollux, one of which has its root meaning 'pure', the other 'polluted'. Gemmation, linked with the name of this sign, refers to propagation by budding, emphasising the connection of Gemini with all young life. The Gemini constellation has a pair of bright stars, both of magnitude 1, which are very close together in the sky.

These two stars to mark the Twins' heads, with one more orange and the other more northerly. The two great stars which bear the names of Castor and Pollux, are situated not more than five degrees from each other and were long known as the sole representatives of the entire constellation. But over time many more stars were added and the brothers 'grew'. Castor is really two very closely placed white stars which revolve around each other, resulting in a 'binary system' effect, the name given by astronomers to the phenomenon of two stars revolving together around a common centre of gravity. The Twins are usually depicted as holding hands or bound together by each other's arms, and are most easily seen in the April sky. They are easy to recognise due to their position behind the constellation of Orion.

WISHING UPON YOUR STAR

The practice of wishing upon a star is familiar to most of us, and is a mystical superstition that is ingrained in many of us from childhood. As a night-time ritual, you can wish upon your own sign's constellation or that of the sign whose energies you wish to call forth; indeed, you can wish upon any constellation you feel an affinity with. If you can't see a particular constellation in your night sky, you can always meditate on it in your mind, or you can use the traditional technique of wishing upon the first star you see, while reciting the popular rhyme: *Star light, star bright, first star I see tonight, I wish I may, I wish I might, have the wish I make this night!* Any one of the three rituals will hold power for your own special wish. Good luck!

THE GEMINIAN SYMBOL ♊

Astrology uses symbols or 'glyphs' to represent the planets and signs. The glyph is made up of shapes representing the energy and physical matter of which the Universe is composed, and how these shapes are used in each symbol provide hints as to the properties of the sign or planet it represents.

The ancient view was that there were five elements: Fire, Water, Air, Earth and Ether (or Spirit). Ether is invisible energy, while the four tangible elements are known as 'matter'. Ether, as pure energy, cannot be influenced by any of the physical/matter elements, although it surrounds them and indeed fuels them. The Greek philosopher and scientist Aristotle regarded this idea as a circle (Ether/Spirit) with a cross (matter) in the centre. This glyph is used in astrology as a symbol for Earth, and the cycle of life. All the symbols used in astrology represent the relationship between energy and the 'matter' elements.

Gemini's glyph looks like the Roman numeral 2 (II). It represents two pillars of wisdom, dual lines of intellect or mentality. There are no curves, meaning it is detached and cerebral. The horizontal line is considered concrete or physical when at the bottom of the glyph, abstract or metaphysical when at the top, therefore Gemini combines these two principles. The vertical lines symbolise destiny or intellect, and represent detachment, objectivity and the unemotional realm; in fact, because this glyph consists entirely of straight lines, it contains no emotional element.

Consisting of these two horizontal and parallel lines linked together by two narrower vertical and parallel lines, they represent the Twins of the zodiac, corresponding to the two stars, Castor and Pollux.

Although essentially implicit of objectivity, Gemini's glyph represents the duality of existence and the possibility of making a choice between good and evil through knowledge arising from the union of spirit and matter. The symbol of the Twins also conveys this same idea of duality. In its highest form, Gemini embodies the principle of the joining together of the rational mind and greater creativity through wise application.

THE AGE OF GEMINI ★ 6000 - 4000 BC

The Age of Gemini is described by historians and astrologers alike as a golden period of intellectualism and progress. It was marked mainly by the development of writing, as humanity began to record information for posterity. Writing began with rough symbols carved on stones, and by the end of this period there is evidence of Chinese and Egyptian cuneiform writing. In some of these writings, the 'Golden Age of Wisdom' was described, and this fell during the Age of Gemini. This period also saw the invention of the wheel, which made rudimentary commerce possible, and transportation vastly improved. Seafaring was also prominent, and trade increased as new routes were opened. The emphasis on communication, travel and writing meant that large territories could be run effectively and profitably. The Age of Gemini also witnessed the beginning of urbanisation, during which great civilisations flourished in Egypt, Mesopotamia and the Indus Valley. The first evidence of organised religion, as well as the concept of libraries beginning to take hold, also date from this period.

THE RUNDOWN & LESSONS
SOME QUIRKS, ODDITIES, UNIQUE CHARACTERISTICS & IDIOSYNCRASIES OF GEMINI

"One way or another, Gemini will triumph with words ... he can sell ice cubes to an Eskimo or dreams to a pessimist."
***Linda Goodman's Sun Signs*, Linda Goodman, Pan Books, 1968**

"What makes Geminis' moods and evasions tolerable is that they are really, really interesting. To some people that might not sound like much. But to those who have had quite enough of dull people leading dull lives, where imagination never takes wing & humour never sparkles, Gemini is like a draught of the elixir. He reminds you that life is new and fun and fascinating. Spend some time around one, and you might even discover you've grown wings yourself."
Linda Goodman

There are two types of thinkers: what I like to call 'right-brainers' and 'left-brainers'. The left hemisphere of the human brain deals with things such as control of speech, verbal functions, reason, logic, mathematics, linear concepts, details, sequences, the intellect and analysis; the right hemisphere is concerned with spatial, music, holistic, artistic concepts, as well as simultaneity and intuition. You could go on to say that the left brain is masculine or yang in quality, and the right brain is feminine or yin in quality. Based upon these very simplistic outlines, it can be further stated that Air sign Gemini dwells mainly in the left hemisphere, with a teensy bit of right thrown in for good measure.

The cerebral nature of Air highlights thought rather than emotion and feeling. Gemini is largely motivated by reasoning processes. Positive, hot, moist, sanguine and rational, an adaptable (Mutable) intellectual (Air) approach characterises the sign of Gemini.

Gemini is the first of the Airy signs, is positive in magnetism, and is ruled by the planet Mercury. Your combination of Air and Mutability makes you one of the most difficult signs to pin down - but also the most versatile. People born under this sign are generally quick, restless, alert, agile and sociable. Gemini likes people - the more the merrier - and always keeps the party swaying. Gemini masters walking and talking, is simple yet intelligent, and responds immediately in thought and speech - sometimes too hastily and superficially, but always changing to adapt to any new information or environments.

Gemini is the snap, crackle pop of the zodiac. With a mind as quick as a whip and a highly independent aura, you talk fast, listen fast and read fast, gathering all the facts you need in mere seconds. If you try to squeeze a glob of the chemical element quicksilver (otherwise known as Mercury) in your hand, it seems to disperse immediately into hundreds of sparkling silver balls that quickly escape through your fingers, no matter how much you try to clasp it. This example epitomises the Twins' spirit. He is quicksilver at its most characteristic and exasperating

- separating, then blending, then separating again ... and on it goes.

Gemini is to the world what the nervous system is to the body. It does not introduce any new information but is a vital transmitter of impulses from the senses to the brain and vice versa. The nervous system does not measure, weigh or judge these impulses - it simply conveys the information, and does so perfectly and efficiently. This analogy offers an indication of Gemini's role in the world. You are the communicator and conveyor of information. To you, the truth or falsehood of information is irrelevant; you only transmit what you see, hear or read about. Therefore, you are capable of spreading the most outrageous rumours and engaging in petty gossip, *as well* as conveying truth and light. Because of this unscrupulousness in your communications, you can do both great good or plain wrongdoing with this power, and this is why your sign is symbolised by the Twins: you have an intrinsically dual nature.

Being a brilliant, sparkling Air sign, Gemini deals within the realm of logic and is strongly connected to the rational world of thought. Bright, breezy, witty, clever and articulate, your Mutable nature shows itself in your adaptability and mobility. You seek to understand links and find excitement in information. Finding it hard to stay focused, a typical Gemini is flighty, restless, easily bored and uncommitted, but also finds it easy to be flexible and adaptable if plans change course. Your character fluctuates and advances so frequently, that you will seek those people or situations who match your interests at the time. Indeed, anywhere you lay your hat is home.

Being an early zodiac sign, and relating strongly to sibling and immediate environment relationships, Geminis' essence is the root of all relationships; it is through these early, younger years that we develop skills in dealing with other people. In the developmental process, it signifies the first time we become 'separated' from others, for example from our first human attachment or caregiver. Gemini seems to have a subconscious (or otherwise) memory and feeling that they weren't always alone - not literal of course, but a 'sense'. Its symbol, the Twins, reflect the thirst for knowledge and experience that all inquisitive children seek. But they are highly strung and impatient and want the knowledge immediately - and all of it. Gemini has the skill to be involved with many different things simultaneously, and you need this variety to fully express your qualities. But you often fail to do anything in depth, because you are clever enough to get away with it.

Your famed flexibility and versatility are a blessing and curse, in that you will bend to almost any wind, but you lack the staying power of the more Fixed signs. Your boredom threshold is irritatingly (to those around you) low and you are constantly on the lookout for new experience and stimulation. Any kind of routine, drudgery or monotony will drain you and lead to resentment or even depression. Your restless Mercurial nature demands constant change and novelty, otherwise your spirit will grow dejected and morose. Restrictions of any kind also stifle you.

Your generally cheerful, friendly nature seeks constant companionship. Naturally gregarious, you hate - even deeply fear - being alone for extended periods of time. However, if anyone tries to repress your spirit in any way, you can become as elusive, changeable and unpredictable as the wind. You know how to love without smothering and possessiveness is simply not part of your make-up. Your friendship has such an Airy, unreachable quality that you seem to lack the Earthy passion of other signs. But your Mercurial temperament and emotional coolness can be warmed considerably if your loved ones share in your ideals, whims and dreams, for it is through mental rapport that you build your strongest relationships.

You will try anything once and although highly intelligent, are rarely profound. Although you may appear to take only a superficial interest in what's going on around you, your agile brain will have skimmed off the salient points from any subject in hand, and to Gemini, the salient points are all that matter. Despite this - or perhaps *because* of it - you are capable of displaying amazing insight and a cutting wit that can catch others by pleasant surprise.

For all your perceptiveness and brightness - you are the fastest wit of the zodiac - you are prone to being impatient of slower-minded people. You rarely give your full attention to anyone or anything. This does not imply a lack of interest, but rather that you are capable of thinking about several things at once and pulling it off with typical aplomb, skill and effortless charm.

There's something of the eternal child about Gemini and most Geminis retain their youthful attitudes and looks well into old age. Sometimes affectionately called the Peter Pan of the zodiac, there's a youthful air of irresponsibility and carelessness about Gemini, no matter what their age. Your restless lifestyle usually ensures your metabolism is high, but you often pay a price with a sensitive nervous system. Almost everything you do is carried out at top speed and you may find it difficult to relax.

Emotionally you are akin to the darting, flitting flight of the butterfly; you lack emotional resilience and empathy, and you are not too comfortable with feelings. You are a cerebral sign who insists on dissecting others' emotions, but tend to hide your own feelings and have little sensitivity or regard for the feeling side of the psyche. But still, there's an eagerness about you, an immediate, sympathetic friendliness that puts others at ease. If you can sit still for long enough, others find yours a wonderful - and uplifting - shoulder to cry on. Indeed, you can cheer the bluest of hearts and chase away the blackest of clouds; there is always a rainbow just under the clouds in Gemini's sky.

Gemini has a reputation for being the trickster of the zodiac, and there is some truth to this. You often have problems knowing exactly what your own truth is and because you so regularly change stories without even noticing, and you find it equally hard to cover your tracks when you tell white lies. You tend to dismiss and discard inconvenient 'truths', especially when you detect an opportunity to manipulate, for you can also be a skilled con artist. Gemini gives an irresistible sales pitch and is an irreplaceable asset behind any perfume sales counter. You will sweet-talk a chair if you have to. And as a promoter of anything, you can be absolutely mind-blowing. The amazing Geminian gift of the gab and facility of speech can make you a brilliant politician, as well as an expert in the field of anything that requires human communication.

As mentioned earlier, Gemini is the communicator of the zodiac, and you are rarely satisfied unless you are talking or exchanging, sharing and gathering information. Your almost unquenchable hunger for knowledge means you are a veritable storehouse of facts and figures and titbits and trivia - and Mercury's influence compels you to pass them on through verbal or written means. Indeed, you are associated with the making of connections, with linking people together within relationships. Your own relationships are likely to be made most easily with those with whom you have an excellent mental connection; if this is lacking, you find it hard to connect and give of yourself. Like your element Air, you prefer to keep your relationships light, breezy, friendly and on the surface. In love you like to remain uncommitted, unencumbered and free, and you may even be still chasing romances well into your middle age. Emotionally inconsistent but ever the charmer, you are an incurable flirt - you fall in love instantly, but you fall out of love just as quickly, which can unsettle more stable or security-seeking types. Being so sociable, communicative, candid and talkative can have its drawbacks, as any Gemini knows. As a sign of relationships, you love to exchange opinions, but when this is carried too far you can become quite a vehement orator. In addition to this, you can be quite a gossip and one of your less desirable traits is your looseness of tongue and consequent untrustworthiness; most Geminis find it difficult to keep a secret.

The connection with the skilled trades is part of the Gemini archetype, for yours is the sign of versatility and dexterity *par excellence*, and in medical astrology Gemini rules the hands, those 'twin' instruments of skill and manual accomplishment.

Restless, entertaining, usually intellectual and always alert, Gemini is the livewire of the zodiac. You are immensely sociable and your circle of friends is likely to be large and wide-ranging. You know how to adapt yourself to fit into any social context. But, your sociability can mislead people into thinking you are always light-hearted, when in reality you actually swing between the highs and lows, as your dual nature indicates. Here one place today, somewhere else tomorrow; breezy and communicative one minute, sullen and acerbic the next; these tendencies can characterise what is regarded by many astrologers as Gemini's two-faced syndrome. Sometimes one Twin doesn't know what the other Twin feels, or even what it is doing, and vice versa.

More than any other sign, Geminis can benefit greatly from meditation and purposeful focus; without channelling your mind properly, you can easily become scattered, wayward, nervous, mischievous, over-excitable, and ultimately ineffective.

The essence of Gemini's duality usually manifests as the interaction between two opposing forces - the light and the shadow, for example, and perhaps most often overlooked, Gemini's desire for 'a place among the stars', accompanied by a yearning for something which is not accessible in physical or Earthly forms. Even the Gemini himself can't pinpoint exactly what it is that is missing - but it is most probably that his soul mate exists on another plane, like the Twins Castor and Pollux upon which much of Gemini's mythology is based, the mortal one having died. There are always two sides to a Gemini, and sometimes one side is missing altogether, which confuses both himself and others, and prompts an eternal search for the 'other self'. But when the duality of Gemini is united and focused, great accomplishments are possible. You are, after all, optimistic, full-of-crackling-energy, smart and devastatingly witty - and since you're represented by the Twins, arguably twice as much fun as anybody else - or is that actually *double trouble*? Such is the life and (mis)adventures of the Twins, who, according to one star-gazer, "skim through life like Pippa passing, always light-hearted, sparkling, laughing, and recording only the sunny hours." You are, after all, the zodiac's little ray of Sunshine - and just like beams of sunlight, you are bright, shiny and refreshing, but something that defies concrete definitions, for the essence of Gemini, like the sunbeam, can never be truly encapsulated.

LESSONS TO BE LEARNED FOR GREATER POWER, ENLIGHTENMENT & LUCK

Gemini problems and ultimate undoing's arise through your manipulative and fickle nature, gossip, superficiality, inability to hold onto a secret (which manifests as untrustworthiness), and your tendency to become bored too easily. Being the trickster of the zodiac, you make an excellent conman, but to say that your innate ability to sell ice to Eskimos and eggs to a chicken farm is an art, is debatable. The motivation behind this is usually boredom, a feeling of superiority, misdirected confidence, a need for attention or a sense of being ignored. While you are a jack of all trades, you are a master of none, because to become an expert in something requires effort, consistent study, perseverance and endurance, all of which you lack due to your constant need and search for fresh stimulation and novel experiences. You need to learn how to stick at things and commit for longer before seeking those greener pastures which promise much but ultimately deliver little. Superficiality can also result from being a jack of all trades, in that nothing is studied, learned or sustained in depth. A broader perspective, deeper insight, making the effort to dig a little further down, and greater staying power all need to be fostered if you are to keep your restless nature in check.

Mental power, logic and reason form the bedrock of Gemini's identity, and these can be your greatest weakness or your greatest strength. Mercury endows you with intellectual gifts and what could be more changeable than the mind? At your best, you observe, gather facts, learn by experience, accumulate information, and arrive at conclusions that are both true and serve you well in your missions. Being an Air sign, you are objective enough to tolerate and allow others their opinions, paths and thoughts, yet firm enough to stick to your own truth, however differing it may be from one day to the next. But reason and rational thinking can also have their pitfalls. Your impressionability and need to belong socially, can lead you to follow bad influences, or deceive and manipulate others, then justify these to yourself. You can happily fly free on the wings of your mind if you can safeguard against these challenges - by thinking, feeling and speaking your inner truths and honouring them with a humbler variety of consistency and integrity.

THE THREE DECANS OF GEMINI

Decans are thirty-six groups of stars that rise in a particular order on the horizon throughout each Earth rotation. These decans were developed in Egypt thousands of years ago. The rising of each decan marked the beginning of a new 'decanal hour' of the night for these ancient people, and eventually three decans were assigned to each zodiac sign. Each decan covers ten degrees of the zodiac wheel, and is ruled by different planetary rulers that rule over the other two signs of the same element (and a traditional ruler, when only seven of the planetary bodies were known). Decans continued to be used throughout the Ages, in astrology and in magic, but many modern astrologers, for whatever reasons, tend to disregard them. Following are brief descriptions for each decan of Gemini. Which one do you belong to? Can you relate to the description and the energies of your decan's ruling planet?

FIRST DECAN GEMINI ★ May 21 - 31

Ruler ★ Jupiter (traditional *) / Mercury (modern)

Keyword ★ Intuitive

First Decan Geminis' Three Special Tarot Cards
The Lovers, Knight of Swords & Eight of Swords

Birthdays in this decan range from 21st May to 31st May. This is the Gemini decan, ruled by Jupiter * and Mercury. Geminians born during this decan possess a restless disposition with a need for adventure, freedom and learning. This influence stimulates intelligence and higher thinking functions, making you a seeker of new experiences and knowledge. Imaginative and inspired, you have sound judgement, great ideas and a high degree of mental receptivity. You may have an interest in the arts, spirituality or philosophy, and most probably love to travel. Mobility is very important to you, and you dislike being restricted or committed in any way, preferring to fly free. Sociable, popular, friendly and creative, you are articulate and clever, but are typically inclined to encounter regular conflicts between your heart and your head.

SECOND DECAN GEMINI ★ June 1 - 10

Ruler ★ Mars (traditional *) / Venus (modern)

Keyword ★ Idealistic

Second Decan Geminis' Three Special Tarot Cards
The Lovers, Knight of Swords & Nine of Swords

Birthdays in this decan range from 1st June to 10th June. This is the Libra decan, ruled by Mars * and Venus. Geminians born during this decan yearn to turn their ideas into realities. Mars, traditional ruler of this decan, activates the intelligence of Mercury, ruling planet of Gemini, making it motivated and driven. Charismatic, creative and charming, you have well-developed communication skills and usually attain any goal you set your high-minded visions upon, due to your astute mind. You thrive in social situations and have a knack for attracting many people to you with your wit, magnetism and style.

THIRD DECAN GEMINI ★ June 11 - 20

Ruler ★ Sun (traditional *) / Saturn (modern)

Keyword ★ Versatile

Third Decan Geminis' Three Special Tarot Cards
The Lovers, Queen of Cups & Ten of Swords

Birthdays in this decan range from 11th June to 20th June. This is the Aquarius decan, ruled by the Sun * and Saturn. Geminians born during this decan are characterised by their versatility, ability to adapt to social situations, quick-wittedness, lucidity and perceptiveness. Although likely to be highly intelligent and showing great leadership skills, you may also possess a narcissistic and egocentric willpower which can take over. You are strong-willed, determined and have the potential to light the way for others due to your immense power and influence. You have vigour and presence, and these, coupled with your original and innovative intellect, make you a force to be reckoned with. Usually flexible and always optimistic, you are a brilliant thinker with an unconventional outlook, drawing people to you with your natural charm. You relish your freedom, and treat every day as an adventure, but due to your restlessness and distaste for being tied down, your character can become diluted by too many pursuits. You are also easily distracted but, being easily bored, your mind is ever open and receptive to new ideas, opportunities and interests.

The decan's traditional ruler based on the Chaldean order of the planets

YOUR ELEMENT ★ AIR

According to the *Oxford English Dictionary*, the word *element* has a mysterious origin, and was first found in Greek texts meaning 'complex whole' or 'a single unit made up of many parts'. From the ancient up to medieval times, there were only four elements - Earth, Air, Fire and Water - and the occult-oriented also believed in a fifth: Spirit, or Ether. (Cornelius Agrippa called Spirit the 'quintessence'.)

Alchemy is a tradition of visions and dreams, and images can combine on different levels of reality. Alchemists have long used images in their illustrations to express the enigma and mystery of their art, and to include all dimensions of our experience. The traditional worlds of Earth, Water, Fire and Air symbolise these dimensions very well. Broadly speaking, and in human terms, Earth corresponds to the level of the body and the senses, Water to the flow of thoughts and feelings, Fire to inspiration and energy, and Air to the world of the higher mind. Each of these worlds has its own realm of imagery. Gemini belongs to the realm of the Air element.

★ The Intellectual Group ★

The path to BROTHERHOOD

Focused on Mental & Social Interactions

Alchemical Associations ★ The Intellect, Gold and the Colour Yellow

Key Attributes ★ Communication, Intelligence, Reason, Perspective, Renewal, Thought, Logic

Symbolism ★ Clear Thought, Communication, Study, Connection to the Universals

Governed by ★ The Mind and the Psyche

Air Characteristics ★ Intelligent, Wise, Thoughtful, Analytical, Detached, Objective

★ THE MAGIC OF AIR ★

Many Eastern philosophies believe that the vital force that energises both humans and the cosmos is carried in the Air, entering our bodies when we breathe. This fundamental energy is called *prana* in India, *chi* in China and *ki* in Japan. Spiritual prayers from Buddhist prayer flags are believed to be carried in the wind.

Air is invisible and intangible, but it drives life and is necessary to animate all living things. Represented by sky, wind, flight and breath, Air can be a cool breeze, fanning the flames of desire, or a strong wind, creating a hurricane. Taking deep breaths can calm and soothe the spirits. Air represents your intellect - the ambitions that are driven by a cool detachment from your emotions. Air seeks out what you need more than what you want and fans you gently along, rather than sweeps you off your feet with the dreams, force or illusions of Water or Fire; Air rationalises your desires. It also refreshes and purifies you, blowing away your problems and carrying you towards new solutions - by being literally a 'breath of fresh air' in your experiences.

★ KEYWORDS ★

Broad-minded, fair, objective, refined, ideas-oriented, communicative, observant, versatile, rational, theoretical, social, learning-oriented, impersonal, logical, innovative, connective, detached, active-minded, clever, curious, impartial, cooperative, abstract, integrating, networking, analytical, relationship-oriented, intellectual.

On Gemini and the Air Element

"In spite of all the people around him, he shares his deepest emotions only with his one constant companion - his other twin self. The Air is his element and his real home. He's a stranger to Earth."
Linda Goodman

Air is the mental principle. The most intellectual and innovative of the four elements, it is unconcerned with the material side of life, but rather it seeks to share with and communicate ideas to others. It is a connective energy, driven to share thought and mental rapport. Air is associated with the thinking function and its motivating force is mind-thought stimulation. Characterised by intellect and aspiration over passion, Airy types are ideas people, using rational and logical thought processes, seeking mental understanding and experiencing life through the mind. They are also objective and 'head-orientated', sometimes to the detriment of their emotions and intuition.

The three Air signs are Gemini the Twins, Libra the Scales and Aquarius the Water Bearer. In the horoscope wheel, Gemini represents personal development, Libra represents interpersonal development, and Aquarius represents transpersonal development. The Air signs, living in world of communication and the intellect, express themselves in these differing ways: Gemini, through its quickness to see both sides of any issue and to create original thoughts from what has been learned; Libra, through its ability to balance many different viewpoints and find a harmonious consensus and keep the status quo; and Aquarius, through its foresight and vision to understand the Universal principles that can be used for the betterment of mankind. The Air signs are masculine in polarity, extroverted in expression, and are aligned with the realms of relationships and connections of all kinds.

Air is perhaps the most misunderstood of the elements, because of its intangible nature and lack of visible manifestation. However, without Air there can be no Fire; Water devoid of oxygen is merely hydrogen gas; and in the absence of Air there is simply no conscious, breathing life. Air represents the insubstantial state of mind of cognisance. As a progressive chain of development, Elemental Air is the final stage of spiritual evolution. Fire is the first creative spark, which coalesces into the nurturing Waters of life and growth, Earth the solid, corporeal plane of existence, but as all life is cyclical and these material states eventually wane and waste away,

Elemental Air remains as the soul-like auric energy or discarnate spirit. Additionally, Air is usually invisible and one only notices its effects when it is directed through another element. Indeed, Air's magical powers can be activated through Fire (smoke), Earth (moving through mobiles and wind chimes for example), and Water (inhalation, steam and vaporisation).

Air gives us life, thanks to that which we breathe in. It is both life- and death-inducing, very real and yet ambiguous. In astrology, the exact moment the newborn inhales its first breath is when we choose to establish the birth chart. But this rhythm of life is also a rhythm of death. In fact, the breath which enables a child to live independently and freed from its cord, depends on a continuous movement. At the other end of life, withholding your breath signifies drawing your last and expiring, or dying. Ultimately, breathing is a spontaneous, instinctive, vital action which allows us to exist.

The soul and breath have always been closely linked. But breath is not the soul; it is its vehicle. Both are unseen and impalpable. Breath is also the vehicle for thought, sound, spirit, speech and language. Air is the same for everyone, yet our breath is unique to us alone. Perhaps that is why those born of the Air element often have a delicate albeit superficial sensitivity to the Air around them, its nuances and temperature, its feel and its nature, its fragrance and its moisture.

Air is also associated with inspiration, ideas and exchange, representing the Divine energies and messages from the gods. Inspired by birds, shamans use spirit flight in their healing ceremonies and rituals. Air can open your mind to new possibilities and allow your imagination to take flight. All cultures have legends of wise 'messengers' descending from the air, such as angels, birds, winged dragons and science fiction aliens, all of whom, it is supposed, have access to higher sources of information than Earth-dwellers. Witches are often depicted flying through the Air on their broomsticks, a symbol of their wisdom and magic. And the sky gods of ancient times were all guardians of arcane studies and were thought to pass on these gifts to the humans who believed in as well as called upon them.

When we work with Air, we think of the Divine breath of spirit, the ability to move through space and time, and the wisdom derived from experience and study. Like the other elements, Air has three manifestations - mental, astral and physical - when used in magic and ritual. We can visualise (mental), request the use of the energy (astral), or physically create the Elemental associations in our experience. Where Earth elemental magic lends itself to manifesting things in a physical form, finding treasure, creating abundance and harnessing the strength within, Air is more of a studious, mental variety: writing and telling stories, sending messages, taking (mental) notes, composing music, studying anything, and clarity of thought. Hermes, the Greek messenger god, and his Roman counterpart Mercury are both associated with the Air element.

The Air element is connected to understanding, intellectual concepts, innovations, insight, mental rapport, technology, synthesising information, ideas, communication, and knowledge. As air has no boundaries, it can be difficult for this element to accept boundaries established by others. It is objective, gives a sense of separation through interdependence, is sophisticated and is linked to the past, present *and* future. It seeks intellectual rapport and stimulation above all else, and has a conscious sense of *knowing*.

This element is detached, impersonal, separate, represents breath and life, is an ideas perfectionist, is judging, assessing, collating, paradoxical, space-seeking, freedom-seeking, flighty, has an approach/avoidance element, develops ways to communicate, is an observer/spectator, gossiper, is an excellent witness to the human experience, is an equality-idealist, is dual-natured in many ways, has difficulty with intimacy, is dissociative in the face of challenge, is aware and conscious, has an urge to relate and 'share', is socially inclined and witty, has perspective, keeps its distance, is changeable, fair, learned, inspiring and opinionated, and has an attitude of "knowledge is power."

Airy temperaments excel at clear, objective reasoning and have a capacity for lively, intelligent communication and the exchange of ideas. These types are gregarious, civilised, curious, cooperative, casual, fun-loving and sociable.

However, they can be overly intellectual, objective and rational, uncomfortable with feelings, and too often trust their heads before their hearts. Other weaknesses that may trip them up occasionally are that they have a tendency to be scattered, unfocused, unrealistic, detached, distant, impersonal, nervous, unstable, inconsistent, spacey, erratic, whimsical, fickle, impractical, superficial, opinionated, dogmatic, impulsive, skittish, 'mercurial', disembodied, a chatterbox, have an overactive mind and can't be tied down.

As the element suggests, Airy spirits are constantly on the move, shifting, changing and evolving. Air signs are generally unnerved by states of flux, as movement is a chance for growth and exploration to these inquisitive souls. Independent, open-minded and spontaneous, Air signs loathe restrictions and anything which curtails their freedom, especially of thought. They love to broaden their horizons through circulating amongst people, places and experiences, as understanding others and their surroundings is paramount to making sense of their existence.

Air signs rely heavily on reason, logic and objectivity. This enables the cerebral Air signs to make fair and objective assessments, but this intellectualisation of thought and feeling can also make them come across as detached and unemotional. As they have a strong need for novel and perpetual stimulation, Air signs tend to be restless and can suffer from nerve-related upsets. But blessed with outgoing and naturally expressive personalities, they are highly sociable as well as good communicators. Air signs enjoy the company of others and love engaging in hearty, interesting conversations through which they can gain knowledge and swap ideas. Impartial by nature, they often make great mediators in relationships or families and having an upbeat, generally uncomplicated nature means Air signs also have a natural talent for diffusing tense situations and lifting the spirits of others.

Positive Air Qualities ★ Focused on ideas and their expression, objective, tolerant, inspiring, articulate, socially adept, intelligent, cooperative, stimulating, charming, rational, relational, mentally clear, succinct, detached, perceptive, sharp, clever, gregarious, and capable of forethought, understanding and the grasping of abstract concepts.

Negative Air Qualities ★ Impractical, unemotional, lacking in sympathy, glib, non-committal, facile, hyperactive, nervous, dissociated from the body and the physical world, manipulative, flighty.

THE ARCHANGEL OF AIR ★ RAPHAEL

An archangel is an angel of greater than ordinary rank. They possess a stronger, more powerful essence than the guardian angels, through overseeing and guiding the other angels who are said to be with us here on Earth. The word 'angel' derives from the Greek word *angelos* meaning 'messenger'. To humans, angels are often seen as bringers as all sorts of messages. Angels in all their forms are believed to bring the message of 'spirit' into matter, carrying the blueprints of creation and the Source from the Divine into the manifest world. Angels are not and never have been human; they, like fairies and nature spirits, are part of a different evolutionary pattern – but they do appear to us in human form (usually with wings) because that is what we understand. An angel can be in many different places at once, and with the same intensity and concentration, and wish for us to be aware of them and benefit from them.

There are said to be three categories of angels in the cosmos, each with three subdivisions *. 'Angel' is the generic term and also relates specifically to those closest to the physical. Similarly, archangel may be taken to mean any of the higher orders, and indeed signifies the order just above ordinary 'angel'. Found in a number of religious traditions, the word 'archangel' itself is usually associated with the Abrahamic religions.

The word archangel is of Greek origin, and means literally 'chief angel'. All archangels end with the 'el' suffix, 'el' meaning 'in God' and the first part of the name meaning what each individual Angel specialises in. The archangel who rules your sign will be the one with whom you most resonate. The astrological sign is an energy signature, a matrix of a specific stellar pattern that will subtly affect and influence you. Although there are many associations for the great archangels of the Universe, we must keep in mind there is great overlapping in their duties and guidance. For example, we may say that one is for healing and another for protection, but they can all perform the functions of the others, and each has only areas of greater focus and responsibilities. Four of the multitude of archangelic beings work intimately with the Earth. These are Raphael (Air), Michael (Fire), Gabriel (Water) and Uriel (Earth). Associated with each of these archangels are one of the four elements, specific colours, one of the four directions or quarters of the Earth, three signs of the zodiac, and a variety of other energies and powers. Understanding these associations and considering them in relation to our own paths, can help us determine with which of them we are more likely to resonate. Your sign, being of the Air element, vibrates to the essence of Raphael.

* The first sphere, the *Heavenly Counsellors*, comprises Seraphim, Cherubim and Thrones. The second sphere, the *Heavenly Governors*, comprises Dominions, Virtues and Powers. The third sphere, the *Heavenly Messengers*, comprises Principalities, Archangels and Angels. Of course, all such classifications are a human construct, a way of placing order upon the unknowable and allowing us to perceive something about which we have no words to express. However, as long as we think of angelic hierarchies as a way of working with celestials, of remembering important attributes, and we are able to imagine and experience these beings, this order of angels will prove useful to those wishing to draw upon their messages and assistance.

★ ARCHANGEL RAPHAEL'S ASSOCIATIONS ★

Element of Air
The eastern quarter of the Earth
The spring season
The colour blue (or blue and gold)
The astrological signs of Gemini, Libra and Aquarius

Raphael, meaning "Healing power of God" or "The Divine has healed," is the archangel of healing and safe travels. This being works to stimulate energies for overall life and success. Raphael awakens a sense of beauty, wonder and creativity which stimulates higher mental faculties. He is the supreme healer in the angelic realm, whose chief role is to support, heal and guide in all matters of health, working to heal people's minds, bodies and spirits so they can enjoy overall peace and wellbeing. Raphael is the Keeper of the Holy Grail.

GEMINI'S ZODIAC ARCHANGEL ★ METATRON

Additionally, each sign is associated with a particular archangel. Such knowledge can help you to build up a relationship with these beings, based upon your strengths and needs. However, no link is rigid, and as you work with angels you will come to develop your own affinities. When invoking a specific archangel, a useful ritual to draw them closer is to light a candle in that angel's colour, burn some oil or incense of its scent, and hold the appropriate crystal while focusing on what you are needing guidance on.

YOUR ARCHANGEL ★ Metatron has been called the bright twin to Sandalphon's (preceding sign Taurus's archangel) darkness. His is the light of revelation. Versatile and bestowing the gift of spiritual illumination to those who are receptive, Metatron may blind those who are not ready to receive this blessing, so he must be approached with an open mind and heart. He enables you to de-clutter your life so you are able to move forward and be freer to develop.

SCENT/OIL ★ Lavender

CANDLE COLOUR ★ White

CRYSTAL ★ Herkimer diamond

THE DEVIC REALMS & AIR ★ EAST: REALM OF THE SYLPHS

"Through magick we do conjure the Elements, evoking unto us the special properties of the Life-force for our learning and our coming-into-light. And yet are there secret paths of knowledge that have fallen from the minds of men ... For the way of Magick is a path to sacred knowledge, of reverence and humility - and the world is a wondrous place. Yet how many amongst us have fathomed these depths?"
Merlin's Book of Magick and Enchantment, Nevill Drury

Deva is a Sanskrit word that means 'shining one'. Devas are the life force within nature, and there are four devic realms - Fire, Earth, Air and Water - which contain ethereal elemental spirits or sprites. Elementals are the building blocks of nature, and close to being true energy and consciousness. The four elements correspond to four different states of matter: energy/transmutation (Fire), gas (Air), liquid (Water) and solid (Earth), which are linked to the four human states of consciousness: inspiration, thought, feeling and practicality. There are four spirits, or elementals, which reside in the devic realms, associated with each element. People have been painting pictures, telling stories and writing about these devic realms for hundreds of years, albeit sometimes through disguised mediums such as fairytales or children's fantasy stories like Tolkien's *Lord of the Rings*. The power of the natural world is easily observed and since ancient times primal forces have been ascribed to various spirit beings. Belief in nature spirits is of such ancient origin and is Universal; cultures everywhere have names or words to describe them. In the sixteenth century, a famous Swiss physician, alchemist and mystic called Paracelsus * defined these beings as 'Elementals', classifying them according to the element of nature they inhabit. There are four main levels of elemental beings: Gnomes (Earth), Undines (Water), Sylphs (Air), and Salamanders (Fire). The fifth element of Ether is the element from which came forth the other four, and Ether, or Spirit, has never been defined in any particular category, and encompasses the aspects and beings of all the other elements.

Elementals are usually benevolent guardian beings or spirits that look after nature's secrets and treasures in whatever part of the natural realm they occupy. They can only be seen or 'felt' by those possessing heightened psychic abilities, yet they can be summoned by those practising alchemy, spells and magic in order to harness the forces of nature for their own particular intentions. In our modern lives, it may seem as though this magic doesn't exist, but the truth is that most of us are simply less in touch with it than ever before. The consequence of this is that we are destroying vast areas of land, polluting waters, creating toxic landscapes, and disrespecting the laws of nature, which often whisper their messages softly. It is therefore important for us to look at the beauty that surrounds us with true appreciation and genuine regard, and to open ourselves up to the magic resides within it. The four devic realms can teach us much about nature; they act as custodians for the four elements, and learning to work with them is a way of attuning to all the energies and beings of nature. Elementals are four-dimensional, and have nothing to obstruct their movements. Therefore, they move as easily through matter as we do through air and space. They do require some contact with humans for their own evolution. Helping to direct them is an overseer, traditionally called the King of that element, and an archangel. Each of these elements is affiliated with one of the four directions and each elemental spirit embodies its own special energy. If you wish to re-connect and re-harmonise yourself by working with nature and its messages and lessons, you could begin by learning a little about your element's realm: Your element is Air, which is connected with the East direction and the realm of the Sylphs.

* Paracelsus is considered the most original medical thinker of the sixteenth century. His belief in supernatural beings, intuition and the invisible causes of illness helped him discover hydrogen and nitrogen. Paracelsus believed that "Elementals are unlike pure spirits for they are mortal, but they are not like man for they have no soul."

★ SYLPHS ★

Sylph is from the Greek *silphe*, and the word means 'butterfly'; these spirits control all winds. Sylphs are fairy-like spirits that inhabit the air, winds and atmosphere as well as high mountain tops (not all sylphs are restricted to living in the air, however). They are probably more closely in line with our concept of fairies and angels than the other elemental beings; and indeed, they work alongside the angels. Always active and extremely quick of movement and sound, Air Elementals are also known to be highly intelligent as they can gather vast amounts of information in a short period of time. They are aloof and detached and usually very subtle in their persuasiveness. People with strong sylph influence or activity often find that sexuality is not high on their list of priorities, and may not understand how it can be so with others. But the sylphs stimulate the expression of the creative sexual drive into other avenues of one's life, such as work or hobbies.

The sylphs are guardians of spring, the direction of the east and the wind. Therefore, they are chiefly concerned with communication, the mind, the intellect and the kingdom of the feathered and winged creatures. As the east is the doorway to new beginnings and the direction through which the sacred circle is always entered, air has a uniquely ethereal, otherworldly, wispy quality to it. It makes its presence felt through its four winds: the north brings cold and withering; the east brings new life and freshness; the south brings vitality and warmth; and the west brings fertility and gentle abundance. Air, and its various components, is our vital life force, enabling us to exist. It also supports that which flies - from birds to human-made technology. It allows fire to burn and for communication with others and with the ether to flow with ease, and stimulates our intellect so we can exercise good reason, judgment and rational thought to enhance our lives. Air makes its home in the heavens and yet it flows freely as a gift for all to share. It moves among us like an unseen visitor, giving us life and strength, and carrying our wishes into the breeze for them to return in the form of free-flowing bounty in our physical world. Air inhabits our hearts, bring joy and wisdom and knowing, and sylphs guard these mind treasures as they are pure spirits of truth and beauty whose ways are not sullied by Earthly restrictions. The King of Air is Lugh or Paralda, its archangel is Raphael, its magickal tool is the athame (which calls down the spirits into form), and its sacred ceremonial stones are Lapis Lazuli, Sapphire, Blue Topaz and Azurite. Perhaps Merlin sums up the sylph realm best: "For these beings are like unto jewels of light, their wings glistening as crystal butterflies in the first Dawn. We may see them in a dance of light upon a leaf or petal, perchance amidst the forest dells or in the hidden glades where few have ventured."

INVOKING THE AIR DEVAS

Sylphs are best contacted in high, open spaces where the wind blows freely. They can be found in wind, clouds, rain, storms, and snowflakes. If you are in need of clearer thought and memory, greater freedom or better communication skills, ask the air devas for their help. They can help guide you if you have an important exam or journey to undertake, if you have to give a speech, or if you are doing anything that requires clear, swift thought and self-expression. To make contact with a sylph, make or acquire a dream catcher. A Native American craft, usually hoop-shaped with dangling beads and feathers, these are designed to 'catch' bad dreams and protect you while you sleep. Dream catchers can be adapted to attract sylphs however, although they can never really be caught, since they embody the essence of liberty and unencumbered flight. Perhaps you could get a new dream catcher for this very purpose, and imbue it with your positive intentions through a special affirmation. When you become aware of your sylph stirring your dream catcher, ask for the specific help you are requiring, thank the sylph for his or her help, then set them free back into their realm of flight and freedom, knowing that their help has been given and their work done. Sylphs also respond well to the burning of incense and music.

THE EAST DIRECTION'S CORRESPONDENCES

If you wish to work more with your particular element and direction, the following may help propel your wishes and magical journey:

Time of Day ★ Dawn
Polarity ★ Male, positive
Exhortation ★ To *will*
Musical Instruments ★ Wind instruments, harp
Colours ★ Gold, white
Season ★ Spring
Magical Instrument ★ Wand
Altar Symbol ★ Incense
Communion Symbol ★ Scent
Archangel ★ Raphael
Human Senses ★ Hearing, smell
Art Forms ★ Poetry Painting
Animals ★ Birds, bats
Mythical Beast ★ Winged horse
Magical Arts ★ Divinations
Guide Forms ★ Sky/weather gods
Meditation ★ Sky, clouds
Images & Themes ★ Mountain tops, flying, sunrise, wisdom and knowledge

HOW YOU CAN GET IN TOUCH WITH YOUR AIR ENERGY

"When we are present with and summon the magic of Air, we gain wings"

★ Use Air energy when making wishes around the following: Travel, exam success and study, job interviews, meditation, relaxation, more effective communication with others, improved expression and articulation of needs, mental stability, increasing knowledge-base, nervous stress relief

★ In magical practices, Air can be represented by smoke, which can be created by burning a joss stick or incense. The following tools and methods can also be used to carry your dreams to the skies and ether: Feathers, hanging mobiles in the breeze with your wishes attached, paper darts, autumn leaves, and airborne seeds

★ The best days on which to employ Air magic are Wednesdays, ruled by the planet of communication Mercury, or Thursdays, ruled by Thor, the Norse god of thunder. If possible, choosing a windy day with gales or thunderstorms will make your work more powerful. Air spells are also most effective when performed beneath an open sky; a high mountain would be an ideal location. Writing a wish on a kite or a balloon and guiding it through the air, as high as possible, by a piece of string can harness the magic of the Air spirits, who will help you clarify and manifest your desires, through quite literally releasing your wish into the wind

★ Spend time in open, fresh, clean air regularly

★ Spend time in wide open spaces and engage in outdoor activities that make use of the air around you, such as flying a kite or ballooning

★ Learn Prana-, Chi- or Ki-related disciplines, martial arts, meditation and yoga that focus on breathing, focus, mental-detachment and concentration

★ Read as much as you can; be an eternal student

★ Blue-coloured crystals will activate your connection with the element of Air and enhance your dreams, soothe your fears, calm your nervous system, help you communicate, bring about inner peace, and assist in self-transformation

★ Develop your networking skills

★ Throw intellectual dinner parties

★ Join a discussion group or an online Internet chat room

★ Practice deep breathing

★ Learn about meteorology, cloud formations, the atmosphere and the weather

★ Use a negative ion machine, humidifier or air purifier in your home

★ Don't smoke, or if you do, quit (being associated with the lungs, Geminis should particularly take note of this)

★ Sleep on an air mattress

★ Meditate on the Swords suit in the Tarot (the Swords suit represents the Air element)

★ Take a course - in anything and everything!

★ Know a little bit about everything; trivia is more powerful than it's given credit for!

★ Write; keep a journal

★ Visit the library on a regular basis; join a book discussion group

★ Look after your lungs, other components of your respiratory system, and your nervous system

★ Take a course, learn a language, or otherwise make a commitment to a learning activity which requires discipline, focus and mental energy

★ Take a course on improving your relationships

★ Hire a jumping castle and invite your friends over!

★ Jump on a trampoline

★ Practice public speaking often, even solo in front of a mirror

★ Forget your mind chatter and allow your heart to lead occasionally; it always knows where to go

★ When working with the Air element in magical practice, stand at the East quarter of your magical space, as the East is its domain, and invite its living essence into your 'circle'

★ Air spirits are also known as air devas, zephyrs, builders or sylphs, and can be called upon to calm our nerves, cleanse our thoughts, clear anxiety and fear, and to help us focus with greater mental clarity, so Air signs would be wise to adopt one (or all) as their very own spirit guide!

YOUR MODE ★ MUTABLE

Each sign belongs to one of the three quadruplicities, Cardinal, Fixed and Mutable. If we closely examine the Earth's yearly cycle, we can form a very accurate picture of the nature of these quadruplicities, for they correspond directly with the manifestation of the seasons. Each season has three months: the first month brings the new phase of the cycle, the second month brings a concentration of the season's energy to its fullest expression, and the third month represents the transition from the current season to the next one. The astrological quadruplicities represent the three basic qualities in all life: creation (Cardinal), perseveration (Fixed) and destruction (Mutable). Every thing that is born, from a period of time to a human being, experiences a life and then dies. In this context, death can be taken to mean that the form of the energy changes; but the energy itself can never be annihilated, for form is mortal, whereas essence is immortal.

The Mutable mode covers the signs Gemini, Virgo, Sagittarius and Pisces, and is the most flexible group of the three modes (the others being Cardinal and Fixed), able to shift and change to facilitate action. You instinctively know how to go with the flow and you adapt most easily to new situations and have diverse interests, but can lack perseverance and are prone to restlessness. Operating with flexibility and mobility, you are adaptable to change and have a circulating quality. Cooperative and friendly, you can fit in almost anywhere, put up with anything and turn any situation to your advantage. You can steer projects through periods of transition and can also bring them to a conclusion, but are conspicuously absent when hard work, long hours or persistent effort is necessary (with the exception of Virgo).

Although gentle, generally easygoing and likeable, you can be childish, sulky and ruthless if threatened. And although you have a natural benevolent streak and love to help animals and people, you can also be paradoxically selfish. The natural versatility of the Mutable quadruplicity can develop into a willingness to change and compromise, which gives an enormous sense of resourcefulness to these signs.

Being so versatile, you are constantly seeking ways you can make improvements to yourself and your life; Mutable signs can always be relied upon to think of new and ingenious ways of dealing with changing circumstances. However, without the proper focus, centralising force, direction or persistence, your energy can become easily scattered, flighty, wavering and disoriented - and thus ultimately ineffective. You often lack a fixity and determination of purpose, which are needed to concretise goals. Your essential energy is one of movement, flow, fluidity, adaptability, adjustability, harmony, and versatility. Your feelings can switch and shift easily and you can be moody, indecisive, inconsistent and unpredictable. And although resourceful and ingenious, you can often project nervousness and worry. You may act as the intermediate between the Cardinal and Fixed signs. Mutable also indicates the ending of seasons, which are times of change and transition, merging into new territories and changing conditions.

Being of the Air element, Gemini is the most communicative and sociable of the Mutable quality; you are constantly seeking to share and exchange your thoughts with others, which you will adapt to suit any social situation.

YOUR RULING PLANET ★ MERCURY

The Great Communicator, Learner & Eternal Student

Planetary Meditation
I am my Earth (my body),
and my Sky (my transcendence)
I am my Sun (my spirit),
and my Moon (my soul)
I am my Venus (my pleasure),
and my Jupiter (my faith)
I am my Mars (my courage),
and my Saturn (my lessons)
I am my Mercury (my thoughts),
and my Uranus (my truth)
I am my Neptune (my dreams),
and my Pluto (my transformation)

"Visualise the guardian of Mercury in swirls of coloured smoke surrounded by herbs and potions, crystals and gleaming phials of jewel-coloured healing liquids, writing in huge books in strange writing. He is ageless, in some lights an earnest young scientist, in others one of the ancient alchemists who have spent a lifetime in study."

Cassandra Eason, *A Complete Guide to Night Magic*, Piatkus, 2002

Each planet has its own distinctive and original meaning which, according to its position in the zodiac, combines with the qualities that are inherent in each of the twelve astrological signs. If a planet is your sign's ruler, however, it exerts a significant influence upon your life, regardless of its birth chart or zodiacal position.

Errant ★ Associated with the Mind, Communication, Intellect, Learning, Transport, Information Transmission ★ 88 Day Cycle

★ KEY WORDS ★

Information, Communication, Movement, Mobility, Intellect, Change, Adaptability, Rational Thinking, Learning, Analysis, Dissemination, Synchronicity, Perception, Inventiveness, Correspondence, Short Trips, Transportation, Eloquence, Knowledge, Assimilation, Cunning, Coordination, Logic, Expression, Interpretation, Thought Deduction, Adaptation.

★ KEY CONCEPTS ★
★ Mental Processes ★
★ Active Intelligence ★
★ Communication & Expression ★
★ The Neighbourhood Experience ★
★ Mind, Logic & Reason ★
★ Short Trips & Travel ★
★ The Movement of Goods & Ideas ★
★ Thieves, Theft, Trickery & Cunning ★
★ Early Education ★
★ Transmitter of the Spiritual to the Material ★
★ Negotiations ★
★ Sales & Marketing ★
★ Youthful Vitality ★

Day ★ Wednesday

Number ★ 5

Basic Energy & Magic ★ Speed, Communication

Colours ★ Yellow, Silver, Blue, Metallics, Mixed Hues, Checks, Plaids

Gods/Goddesses/Angel ★ Hermes, Mercury, Raphael
Metals ★ Quicksilver, Zinc

Gems/Minerals ★ Citrine, Agate, Opal, Beryl, Tiger's Eye, Topaz

Trees/Shrubs ★ Hazel, Forsythia, Filbert, Myrtle, Mulberry
Flowers/Herbs ★ Bittersweet, Fern, Lavender

Wood ★ Beech

Fabric ★ Linen

Animal ★ Monkey, Magpie, Hare

Element ★ Air

Zodiacal Signs ★ Gemini, Virgo

Zodiacal Influences ★ Rules Gemini; Exalted in Virgo; Detriment Sagittarius; Fall Pisces

"Deep inside his searching, impatient nature, the Gemini seeks an ideal, and his chief problem is in recognising what it is ... Money, fame, wealth, love

and career are never quite enough. Mercury calls Gemini higher and higher."
Linda Goodman

Mercury is the smallest planet and as one of the closest to the Sun is the fastest in its orbit. Mercury was named after the Roman winged messenger of the gods, and known as Hermes to the Greeks. He traversed the land as a messenger between the heavens, Earth and the Underworld, carrying a caduceus, a rod entwined with two serpents that could induce sleep and bring healing. Mercury was said to be the son of Jupiter in mythology, and through his dexterity, communication skills and quicksilver intellect, Mercury came to rule over medicine, commerce, and then later science and technology.

Mercury was discovered around 5,000 years ago, and was one of the five known ancient planets.

This versatile and variable planet has a duality which shows in the signs it rules. It governs Gemini, the sign of immediate relationships (positive expression), and Virgo, the sign of analysis and discrimination (negative expression). The extrovert Gemini and introvert Virgo are two sides of the same essential function - the way we communicate and move, and the way we discriminate and think. Practical, analytical, methodical, determined and deliberate is the way Earthy Virgo will express its Mercurial nature. In Virgo, Mercury denotes the reality principle. It expresses thoughtfully and with consideration for the facts, is stable-minded, not easily swayed by emotion or passion, and has an essentially practical, sensible and focused thinking style.

Connected to writing, speech, journalism and information-gathering, Mercury represents the power of communication, interpretation and self-expression, intelligence, reason, the ability to perceive relationships and connections, and to gather facts, mobility, adaptability to environment, siblings, young people, writers, travellers, speakers, students, teachers, editors and transport workers. It tells us about our intellects and the way in which we express our ideas, and also how we relate to and deal with our siblings, neighbours, neighbourhood (the area in which we live, our place in it and how we interact within it), and immediate environment. Overall, its action is to quicken, enliven and add mobility.

In Gemini, Mercury expresses itself as an experimental, eloquent, jubilant, open-minded and sometimes scattered way of thinking, always mind-oriented, covering a lot of ground and sharing and exchanging what it has 'discovered'. Without taking into consideration other modifying factors within the chart, a Gemini Mercury is conversational, intellectual, sociable and happy to share ideas with others on a wide variety of subjects.

The Egyptians saw Mercury as Thoth, transporter of souls, the conductor of sleepers to dreamland and souls of the dead to Hades, while the Greeks and Romans saw him as Hermes and Mercury, the messenger of the gods. Always pictured with wings on his feet, to represent the speed of thought and the ceaseless activity of the mind, Mercury symbolises all things intellectual and linked with communication. In some mythology, he is a direct descendent of Hermes, the messenger of Zeus, and the god of travels. The deity of roads, protector of travellers, god of doorways, commerce and thievery, of good and bad luck, of treasure troves, of honest and dishonest gain, Mercury is widely known as a thief and a cunning trickster. Using the nimble wit for which Mercury was noted, he was an immortal go-getter, a lightning flash whose mental frequency was always switched to 'high', a god who got things done. This is how we interpret Mercury's role in astrology. If we think of doorways and roads, and forces which channel, direct and concentrate energy from one source to another, we can begin to form a picture of how Mercury works. Mercury gathers the energy from any information we attract, and compresses it into usable form; it can be likened to the wire through which the current flows. As such, it encourages listening and responding, learning and reflecting.

However, Mercury's charm, quick wit, speed, fluidity and cleverness requires positive direction, for he can just as easily turn into a prankster and cheat as into a brilliant scientific genius. Pure Mercurial intellect needs to be humanised, to connect with something worthwhile and significant, to discover lofty purpose, otherwise it can lose itself in the frivolity of its own emotionally detached efficiency (when operating through Gemini at least).

Mercury symbolises the eternal and willing student, highlighting all channels of language, interpretation, reflection, verbalisation, perception, study, teaching and writing. It indicates our urges and levels of interest in exploring and sharing ideas with others, and is also connected with networking.

Mercury relates to our education (particularly early education), our early learning experiences, the foundations of learning rather than abstract thinking, principles of interchange, relatedness, seeing links and connections, and how we use our knowledge and skill to function and articulate effectively. The planet in closest aspect to Mercury is the most important as Mercury is very much coloured by its contacts with other planets and by the sign it is in. Mercury is the bridge between our inner selves (Sun) and the people we wish to share with (Venus). People with a strong Mercury in their chart are quick thinkers and fast talkers, often intelligent and learned, can think and talk too much and have a lot of nervous energy with a sensitive nervous system, and are likely to be interested in writing and journalism, communications, social networking, and information-gathering.

Astronomically, Mercury is the swiftest moving of the independent planets and makes rapid changes of declination in the sky. At inferior conjunction (when Mercury lies between the Sun and the Earth), its magnetic field deviates the stream of electrified particles emitted by the Sun; these particles have an influence on the nervous systems of living organisms on Earth, hence astrological tradition linking Mercury's with the nervous system in medical astrology. Mercurial types, such as those with a strong Mercury placement, or those born under its rule, i.e. Geminians and Virgoans, are prone to restless energy and tend to be nervous, neurotic, flighty or frequently suffer from other types of nervous disorders and disturbances.

In medieval astrology works Mercury was a significator of youth and young people, and those with a strong Mercury, Gemini or Third House in their birth chart, often seem to be 'Peter Pans', possessing a glittering, lively charm and never quite growing up. This youthful quality may mark a highly creative, inquisitive person, or a completely undeveloped naïve individual - sometimes both. Such is the trickery of Mercury. Jungian analysts call this personality type the *puer aeternus*, the 'eternal boy', and indeed having all the innocence of children, these characters' float effortlessly through life with no noticeable purpose or direction.

Mercury is the closest planet to the Sun and therefore completes its revolution most speedily, linking it with speed and haste. Ancient people rarely saw Mercury in their skies, and when they did it was for a brief period of time. Since it can never be more than 28 degrees from the Sun, it is only when it is farthest from the Sun that it can be seen for scant amounts of time just before or after sunset - and due to its close proximity to the Sun, it can never be seen in the night sky, being swallowed by the Earth alongside its Solar neighbour.

Being prominent in your chart as your ruling planet, Mercury gives Geminis a quick wit, ingenuity, adaptability, humour and a love of study and argument. If it is disharmoniously aspected, however, it can give you a changeable, cunning or exaggerating mind, a nervous and excitable temperament, and a tendency to be quarrelsome, superficial or indecisive.

As your ruling planet, Mercury gives you good mental ability, quickness, ingenuity and some secrecy or slyness. You are inquisitive but rather superficial and restless, and a good talker, often more head-based than heart-based. But what you lack in passion and emotion, you more than make up for in bubbly mercurial effervescence.

Like its namesake, those quicksilver globules that are ever-moving and never still, Mercury is a hard one to pin down. Three of its main keywords - communication, intelligence and knowledge - are equally difficult to define. The actual process of communication is a complex series of skills, emotions, experiences and other human capacities that defy simple or universally-accepted description. The mechanisms may be there for communication, but nothing can really happen until they are activated by some impulse, like an electrical current. This is where Mercury comes in. Intelligence is also tricky and indefinable, for through the senses Mercury may pick up and transmit signals to the mind which then trigger feelings and mental programs and 'files' lodged in the brain, but it is neither intelligence nor the mind itself per se, but the *current* that makes the mind work. Mercury is not knowledge either, but the means by which it is collected, codified, deciphered and dispersed. So although these three words are associated with Mercury, the planet's nature itself is really more nebulous than any of them, as it is the facilitator, the fuel that brings the mechanisms of the mind to life, the measurer of circumstances and the digester of meanings. In short, Mercury is a two-way street, linking the external environment with our minds and vice versa.

Mercury can also be likened to a chameleon, changing its colours to suit its surroundings and, being rather neutral itself, is very influenced by the sign and the house in which it is found in the birth chart. Associated with quickness, astrologers have always examined the speed of Mercury to determine the speed or agility of a person's mind or thought patterns. The slow-moving, stationary or retrograde * Mercury describes a slower intellect, people who take longer to come up with answers and solutions, working things out slowly and carefully, while those with a faster-moving Mercury are quick to answer and possess minds which move at great speeds and are one mind-step ahead of everyone else.

The Greeks called this innermost planet 'the twinkler', and it is easy to see how appropriate this name is from the astrologer's point of view.

The glyph (or symbol) for Mercury is a complex symbol, open to various interpretations. It appears as the cross of matter sitting below the circle of spirit, surmounted by the crescent of soul. This stands for the triumph of mind over matter, as in an intellect that can channel energies from above and below. In essence, this emblem stands for active intelligence. The combination of the crescent, the circle and the cross, shows receptivity resulting from the exaltation of spirit over matter, which you are destined, if you haven't already, to master. This icon suggests manifested (crescent) spirit (circle) over matter (cross), and indeed, Mercury's function is to link the spirit to everyday matters to facilitate this process.

Another well-known symbol for this planet is the caduceus of Mercury, which depicts two serpents coiled around a magic wand or herald's staff whose heads are facing each other. On top of the wand or staff is often a pair of wings and a circle, again symbolising spirit. This symbol attests to Mercury being a giver of the healing arts, and it is still used today as the emblem of modern chemists and the medical profession. The caduceus is a complex symbol, but in simple terms it represents the power of wisdom which can bring happiness and good fortune. It protects messengers, who traditionally carried it, as well as its associations with health and healing.

In medieval times, Mercury was also known as Mercurius, the god of the alchemists. Mercurius is 'the alchemical androgyne', lending the astrological Mercury an androgynous quality, that is neither male or female. As Mercury has neither a feminine or masculine energy to it, it is neutral and objective, and works in accordance with its aspects to other planets, its brothers and sisters, effectively plugging itself into their forces and being driven by the resulting power. (According to a Greek myth, the union of Hermes and Aphrodite produced the being known as hermaphrodite, who was both male and female).

The mind itself, which Mercury is said to represent, is beyond masculine and feminine polarities, although it could be asserted that the rational or analytical aspect of the mind may possess a masculine flavour, for the hemispheres of the brain have a distinctly male (right) and female (left) quality. But the entire spectrum of the mind that Mercury encompasses, is a different concept altogether, for it seems to transcend these separations. This can be illustrated by the fact that in some Tarot decks, the Magician card is depicted as Thoth or Hermes. He stands before the four elemental symbols which represent the four functions of the human psyche - thinking, feeling, intuition and sensation. Mercury, the true alchemist of times past, possesses the ability to unite these elements into a single whole. But the power to separate and regroup positive and negative impulses in such a way as to bring you what you want and send away what you don't want is not restricted to magicians. It is available to us all and we are constantly making use of it, either consciously or unconsciously.

The Sun and Mercury's relationship describes the intellect's link with a sense of direction, purpose and will. If these factors marry up harmoniously, the individual's expression will come forth accordingly. It is believed, however, that when Mercury forms too close a conjunction to the Sun, it can metaphorically 'combust', and burn out. The two can also produce too intense an energy, so it is arguably more desirable for them to occupy different signs, or at least be as far away from each other as possible so that the energies of both signs can more easily complement each other by virtue of their distance and consequent objectivity. However, having said this, a close conjunction can just as easily signify a powerful focus of that sign's qualities. Further, one's intellect may be somewhat detached from one's central purpose if Mercury is at its maximum distance from the Sun, but in the case of a close conjunction it can symbolise that the mind and will are united. Mercury, as the smallest and nearest planet to the Sun, and a symbol of the rational mind, is intimately linked with our sense of spiritual direction (the Sun).

There seems to be a strong link between Mercury and Uranus. Uranus, according to esoteric astrologers, is the 'higher octave' of Mercury, and is the archetype of rebelliousness, the inventor, the bohemian, and any relationship between it and Mercury will reveal a person's attitudes towards traditional thought. The well-aspected Mercury-Uranus type is stimulated and spurred on by progressive technology, especially that which advances the speed and style of communication, and seeks to forge new pathways of thought, after shattering any boundaries to mental growth. When teaming up with Uranus, Mercury's powers are intensified, for Mercury likes also to improve things, to add to Universal knowledge through inventions. A planet of progress through experimentation, Mercury is never satisfied by established, ingrained thought and rather is ever seeking new avenues for his agile mind to explore.

A symbol of the rational mind, Mercury is intimately linked with our sense of spiritual direction (the Sun), in that our mind must serve our sense of purpose. In its evolved manifestation, it relates to how we transform our spiritual energies into matter. Mercury affects the transmission of information from one point to another, thereby aiding or interfering with the thought process, communications, technology and travel. Other functions influenced by Mercury include modes of travel as well as commerce, including sales, bartering, negotiating, contracts, importing and exporting. Physically, Mercury governs the hands and fingers, meaning that those with a prominent Mercury in their birth chart will have advanced fine motor skills and probably use hand gestures a lot when talking. Others may have good dexterity, beautiful handwriting or exhibit strong mechanical abilities.

Unlike its high-minded Solar system companion, the planet Jupiter **, which represents one's faith and beliefs systems, Mercury has no in-built bias, nor is it concerned with principles or ethics. Mercury is completely amoral and deals solely in rationale and concepts. It can be likened to the postal officer who delivers your letters; he or she is not responsible for the writing of the letters, nor the contents or the reactions they engender; Mercury, like the postal officer, simply operates as a neutral medium for the interchange of information.

Mercury governs our intelligence, our intellectual approach, learning styles, how we perceive things, and our subjective understanding of ourselves. Having established a sensitive contact with the world, we then try to understand it and make our own interpretations of what we see. We then use our intelligence to express this perception - intelligence being a tool for expression and communication. Our intellect is also a very key feature in our relationships with others.

Mercury is associated with manuscripts, registers, puns, conferences, speaking, buying, employees, busybodies, stammering, reports, questions, short journeys, atlases, stenographers, diaries, maps, scholars, education, speech, ideas, spokesperson, post offices, reason, pens, servants, contacts, statistics, topics, psychiatry, research, skill, dictation, investigation, schools, journalists, publishers, criticism, pencils, school pupils, libraries, dictionaries, mentality, deliveries, scripts, merchants, selling, apprentices, decisions, signs, messages, proverbs, speed, details, language, envelopes, desks, mind, information, boys, quotations, trains, mouth, trade, porters, reading, interviews, invoices, relatives, stationery, labels, secretaries, telephones, writers, testimony, words, textbooks, wit, whispering, walking, vouchers, cablegrams, signatures, letters, names, conversation, announcers, patterns, narrators, neighbours, instruction, nervous, calculations, cabs, publishers, traffic, pickpockets, statements, inquiries, knowledge, news, newspapers, signals, brainy, notes, short travels, records, stamps, translation, hands, dexterity, novels, correspondence, shorthand, intellect, thought, vehicles, typists, vocabulary, interpreters, lectures, diaries, coupons, literature, couriers, drafts, posters, editors, petitions, visitors, logic, prose, mail, encyclopaedias, observations, errands, essays, explanations, facts, billboards, cars, handwriting, autographs, tutors, fiction, files, fingers, tellers, books, commentators, gossip, the press, buses, grammar, graphology, inspectors, telegrams, catalogues, transport, keys, voice, bicycles, learning, linguists, bills, chatter, printing, luggage, biographies, twins, lungs, tongue, magazines, theories, clerks, manicures, advertisements, stories, certificates, arms, young people, auditors, charts, advice, agents, ambassadors, pamphlets, streets, broadcasting, clever, business matters, periodicals, columnists, talking, communication, orators, papers, witnesses, study, comprehension, pairs, writing, concentration, typewriters, respiration, tales, restless, rhymes, roads, rumours, satire, teachers and youth. I'm sure you get the idea!

This Mercurial energy and influence, throughout your whole life, gives Geminis the gifts of versatility, sharp perceptive skills, adaptability, intelligence, reason, cleverness and inquisitiveness. Too much of this Mercurial energy can make one restless, critical, superficial, lacking in imagination, argumentative, inconsistent, non-committal, insubstantial, cynical, immature, overly mind-based, neurotic, nervous, tense, flighty, unreliable, and unable to see the forest for the trees. But the Geminian's key phrase is "I Think," and your thoughts are always off in the sky somewhere flying high as a kite in the Airy substance your element is made of, never quite touching the ground of Earthly practicalities. How will *you* use your phenomenally powerful Mercurial influence?

* Retrograde means that these planets appeared to be travelling backwards at the time of birth. Despite the fact that this is only an apparent phenomenon, a planet in retrograde motion tends to internalise its effect and direct its energies inward. Its energy is internalised and sometimes suppressed, rather than expressed externally. Retrograde planets indicate energies that function in an indirect, ineffective, compulsive or other unconscious manner. Even though all the planets but the Moon and Sun will go retrograde for a period of time, it is Mercury's retrogradation (three times a year for approximately three weeks at a time) that has a earned the reputation as a time when everything gets a little chaotic, especially around communication, travel plans and correspondence. While Mercury is not responsible for the breakdown of its associated correspondences, such as computers, phones, air travel, fax machines, commerce and information services, there is a widespread notion that these breakdowns most often happen when Mercury is retrograde.

** The relationship between the mind and will is imaged mythically by the relationship between Mercury and Jupiter. Jupiter serves to focus one's consciousness. It could be said that Mercury is the servant of Jupiter, i.e. the intellect must be directed towards a higher purpose.

A VERY BRIEF MYTHOLOGY OF HERMES

In mythology, Hermes was the son of Zeus and was renowned as a prankster. The legend tells us that he was born at dawn and by noon he had slipped away from his mother to explore the world. He found a discarded tortoise shell, stretched three strings of plaited grass over it and invented the lyre, and whenever his mother tried to scold him he would charm her by playing sweet music on this beautiful instrument. From then on, Hermes would be involved in much mischief, but always seemed to charm his way out of anything with his cunning, wit, eloquence and persuasiveness. His legacy arguably lives on in the sign of Gemini, and to a lesser degree, Virgo.

YOUR HOUSE IN THE HOROSCOPE ★ THE THIRD HOUSE

Ruled by Mercury, the Third House indicates your logical mind, conscious thought processes, your speech, how you write, and how you express yourself in other forms of communication. It has a strong link with early education, siblings, your immediate environment and neighbours, as well as your neighbourhood and community.

A house is one of the twelve sections dividing the terrestrial globe, viewed from a precise time and geographical place, into sectors from the poles to the horizon. The horoscope, or birth chart, is divided into these twelve sections called houses. Each house governs a different area or 'department' of life, such as relationships, career, leisure and even karma. The reason for this division of the Earth into houses can be understood when we consider that the Sun's rays affect us differently in the morning, at noon and at night, and also in summer and winter, and if we study the cause, we will readily observe that it is the angle at which the ray strikes us or the Earth which produces that difference in effect. Similarly, with the stellar rays, astrologers have observed that a child born at or near midday, when the Sun's rays strike the birthplace from the Tenth House, has an improved chance of public or career advancement in life than one born after sunset. By similar observations and tabulations, it has been found that the other planetary rays affect the various departments of life when their ray is projected through the other houses, and therefore each house is said to 'rule' or govern certain departments of the human life experience.

The Third House, ruled by Gemini, is the house of communication, mental activity, speech, siblings, local journeys and the immediate environment. It is also associated with neighbours, networks, how we speak and listen to others, mechanical dexterity, transport, early education, study, routine interactions, intellectual endeavours, correspondences, conversations, and short distance travel.

The Third House encompasses the early learning environment and shaping of mental patterns, and consequently, your everyday thinking, your basic communication systems, your personal style of communication in speaking and writing, your early schooling from pre-school through high school, your immediate environment or neighbourhood, and your relationships with the people in them. It governs travel over short distances or for short periods of time. Planets in this house can tell us about our early learning, learning style, how we absorb information, our level and type of intelligence, and how we express our intellect.

This house is perhaps best known for its connection to your intellect, thought processes, perception, analytical skills, approaches to learning and absorbing information, style of self-expression, overall mental activity, and the written and spoken word, and all forms of communication - mental and physical - such as mail, newspapers, letters, writers, magazines, advertisements, contacts, agents, your car, phone calls, public transport, errands, discussions, interviews, deliveries, debates, conferences, chatter and rumours. It tells you about the type of mind you possess, your mental interests and attitudes, habits of thought, and general attitude to people and circumstances.

Whatever our culture, our knowledge, the environment in which we grew up and our social background, we all have our beliefs, preferences, ideas, styles, convictions and ideals. They have an influence over the way of life we have chosen, our lifestyle, our tastes, our choices, and undeniably, our exchanges and relationships with others. Such is the greatest principle of the Third House, as it tells us about the mentality of the individual, the way he thinks and the behaviours that emanate from this. It is within the context of our personal thinking style that we take a stand, understand, express, share, exchange, absorb and transmit the information we receive. Somehow, whatever our level of intellect or mode of expression, we never become truly detached from our heritage and roots, but the Third House colours our personal background somewhat with our own unique, unconditioned perceptions and viewpoints.

This House also relates to close relatives (such as aunties, cousins, uncles), and everyday affairs and minor business dealings. It symbolises our first experiences of relationships outside of our parents, and the planets within or sign on the cusp of this house explain how we experience our place in the familial sibling sub-system. It also signifies our first move away from self-absorption, or from putting our own needs first. In this house we find ourselves in the context of a familial environment, engaging with others in a more meaningful, albeit superficial way, in order to develop our place in the wider, social world and to enhance our learning.

The Third House is associated with connections, sequencing and compartmentalising, making sense of our immediate surroundings and how we react to and interact to this environment. The Third House enables us to gather facts and pieces of information, but the Ninth House synthesises this into a whole and gives it significance and meaning. The sign and planets placed here either facilitate or restrict the flow, and the sign on the cusp indicates whether communication will be inhibited or clear, and how easy it is to learn and utilise information. Linked to the rational, logical left brain (the Ninth House being more abstract thought), the Third House describes the concrete function of a person's mental processes.

YOUR OPPOSITE SIGN ★ SAGITTARIUS
WHAT YOU CAN LEARN FROM THE ARCHER

If we look at the zodiac, we can see that it can be broadly divided into two hemispheres, this division being based on the natural division of the year by the two equinoxes. Astrologers often refer to the first six signs, the hemisphere in which the day predominates (the days being longer in the spring and summer months), as the Personal Sphere of Experience, and the second six signs, the hemisphere in which nights are longer, as the Social Sphere of Experience. These two halves of the zodiac perfectly balance and complement each other, and each individual 'personal' zodiac sign has something to teach it's directly opposite 'social' zodiac sign. To generalise, the signs of the personal sphere tend to experience life through a type of self-projection and self-interest which is often socially uncomplicated, unsophisticated or naïve. Their objective is to learn greater social awareness and thereby integrate themselves with the larger, more Universal human collective. On the other hand, the signs of the social sphere are prone to experience life through the use of their more developed social consciousness. In essence, the personal signs (Aries, Taurus, Gemini, Cancer, Leo, and Virgo) usually provide stimulation and new energy to their environment, while the social, more Universal signs (Libra, Scorpio, Sagittarius, Capricorn, Aquarius, Pisces) provide experience, opportunities for wider expression, and give a more broad-minded approach and perspective to their surroundings.

Each sign in a pair seeks and is attracted to the qualities of its complementary opposing sign. Gemini seeks to develop the breadth of vision and philosophical outlook embodied by Sagittarius, while Sagittarius wishes for the alacrity and methodology of Gemini. Gemini dwells within the realm of the distribution of *individual* concepts and ideas, while Sagittarius resides within the realm of the distribution of *social* concepts and ideas.

Although the word 'opposite' conjures up feelings of separateness and differences, the astrological polarities should not be seen as two signs in conflict with each other - their positive expression is to create a natural balance and equilibrium. Each sign has something to learn from its opposite, but also has a contribution to make towards the other sign's more evolved expression. The Third (Gemini) and Ninth (Sagittarius) House polarity is concerned with the immediate environment versus expanded horizons. In fact, the Ninth House is an extension or expansion on the Third House in almost every way: short-distance travel - long-distance travel; early education - higher and further education; direct communication and information - deeper philosophies and exploration; *gathering* information and facts - *seeking meaning in* information and facts. The two balance each other, because the practical immediacy of communication indicated by the Third House is needed if the deeper Ninth House ideas are to be understood.

Positive and Mutable, this polarity is concerned with the mind and knowledge and how it is acquired and expressed. Gemini is preoccupied with knowledge. Facts are a fascination for Gemini and they are an expert at gathering them. But facts without any cohesion are useless, and Sagittarius can teach Gemini how to see the bigger picture and put them into a much more meaningful *whole*. Gemini's greatest tool is his rational mind. Gemini is the intellectual and potential transmitter of Universal ideas, but more often than not the Twins stop at the level of intellect and do not pursue these thoughts into a higher realm. Sagittarius can therefore teach Gemini to make greater use of his mind, bringing the height of wisdom to Gemini's vast storehouse of often indiscriminately-collected information, thereby allowing the whole picture to be seen more broadly and understood intuitively.

Jupiter is the higher octave of Mercury, and yet Gemini can conversely help Sagittarius by bringing the ideals and visions down into the real, practical world of everyday life. Communication is a two-sided process and Gemini can sift the information so that it is easily assimilated by other members of the human race. If Gemini can learn from the Archer the value of higher thinking, he will be the bestower of great gifts upon others, giving them the ideas and principles needed to evolve, being able to explain these concepts through a choice of words that communicates to anyone. Through the lessons of the wise Archer, the Twins can find the exact way of expressing themselves in order to uplift all those around them through the acuity and precision of their thought processes.

Sagittarius is aware of the future, is planning, gains perspective, is assimilating, processes and conceptualises one's perceptions, develops an understanding and wisdom, seeks meaning, is enlightened, is concerned with attitudes and theories, is philosophical, thinks deductively (general opposed to particular), transcends reason, is open to revelation, is religious, moral and concerned with principles and ethics, is purposeful, pursues a meaningful direction, is over-extended, gets carried away with an activity, reaches out, gets swept away by relationships, is teaching, guiding and mentoring, and keenly engages in philosophical discussions.

The Sagittarian follows a different pattern of thinking to Gemini, standing out by his convictions, which are his own, formed from long, profound searches for the truth from many sources. Essentially, the Sagittarius spirit will seek to expand his geographical, intellectual, psychological and spiritual horizons based on his findings. From the much broader-minded Sagittarian, Gemini can learn to focus on one task at a time (as well as delve into it more deeply) and develop its flowering more fully. Gemini also has much to learn from his complementary opposite about transcending superficiality. You can often be overwhelmed by decisions, as you are prone to having too many pots on the boil, too many balls in the air, and a myriad of inner identities fighting for a voice within. No wonder the Gemini mind is often confused; with so many projects on your daily To Do List, it is easy to see why you never know if you're Arthur, Martha or McCarthur. Sagittarius's innate breadth of vision can assist you with this. Although restless and flighty also, Sagittarius has a greater ability to focus on the task at hand, giving it a broad sweep of time and energy. The Sagittarian way of doing things is more discerning and mature than the scatterbrained Gemini's approach.

The inquisitive, intellectually attuned individual, adept at recognising facts and differentiating information through categorisation (Gemini) seeks to understand the intuitive connections and associations between facts and weld them into a meaningful broader whole picture (Sagittarius). The intuitive and broad-minded individual, with a sense of the overall meaning and pattern of life (Sagittarius) seeks to understand the specific ideas and facts which will enable him to communicate his vision in understandable and articulate terms to others (Gemini).

In summary, it could be said that Gemini's native Third House is that of short journeys, frequent trips, daily comings and goings, and Sagittarius's opposite Ninth House is that of long journeys, explorations and adventure. Similarly, the Third House tells us about the nature of one's practical mind and its immediate application, his routine thinking patterns and his habitual mentality, whereas the Ninth House informs us about the manifestation and expression of his higher self, what is going to drive him to probe a subject or idea, and how he would abandon some of his habits of mind or lifestyle for another which may be strange, foreign or in some way different in order to stand by his moral convictions. The Third House is where he receives 'here and now' information, and how he communicates that information; in the Ninth House, this information comes from somewhere else, perhaps his higher spirit, or maybe from distant horizons, perhaps philosophical or spiritual, which stretch out further in both space and time. In essence, the Third House is where the individual's mind has its roots and origins, and the Ninth House is where this acquired mind takes flight to loftier planes. These comparisons gives important clues as to what the Twins can learn from the Archer.

The Gemini's immense world of ideas needs to be brought to the fore and shared with others more authentically, especially those who share your naturally inquisitive and questioning outlook on life. You also need to commit deeper and more strongly to things and people that you believe in, as you have a tendency towards boredom and changing activities as soon as they become a chore. You live a lot in your head, in the world of ideas and thoughts, but for your soul to truly dance, you need to be more broad-minded and develop stronger and deeper belief systems. If you are a true Gemini, your beliefs and viewpoints are probably quite changeable; Sagittarius can teach you how to nurture stronger, more fixed convictions and then to live by that code.

Geminis have an abundance of powerful social charisma and are very likeable and popular, but your incessant chatter and insignificant talk need to be kept in check. Be more mindful about what you talk about. Eleanor Roosevelt sums up the

Gemini/Sagittarius divide perfectly in her quote: "Great minds discuss ideas; average minds discuss events; small minds discuss people." Although you are indeed capable of profound intellectual expression and exchanges, you often engage at the lower levels of 'small minded discussions' about mundane issues, trivial matters and other people. Sagittarius can teach you how to raise yourself to that higher level, where great minds sit around kingly tables enjoying expansive conversations and discussing concepts that enhance both personal and collective spiritual evolution.

Gemini can be likened to a will-o'-the-wisp, friendly and sociable, but his relationships have a superficial slant to them. He is interested in everything but he never does anything in depth, and is reluctant to commit himself or to follow a particular venture to its end. Likewise, he is afraid to commit lest it leads to a loss of personal freedom and mobility; he is inquisitive but muddle-headed and flittery; and in social interactions he is not always sincere. The Sagittarian on the other hand, oozes charm *and* sincerity, teaching the Gemini that you can - and should - possess both qualities at the same time. Gemini doesn't mean to be insincere, it's just that it's second nature to use trickery and subtle manipulation in his dealings with people. Sagittarius employs honesty and truth, and although often brutal and direct in their delivery, could never be accused of telling untruths. Gemini will tell white lies for a game, never to hurt anyone intentionally, or as a means to get ahead in the business of life. The Archer can indeed teach you how you can be honest and *still* win the race. So in conclusion, you can be charming and sincere, *and* honest and successful. Just ask the Archer. He lives by his truth and can teach the cunning Twins how to also.

Sagittarius is well aware, through all his philosophical explorations and questing, that the grass is always greener just over the horizon. But the Archer will enjoy the often vast journey to get there, while you will simply jump the fence in search of your quick fix.

Geminis have the ability to conceptually encompass wider horizons and this is what you must begin to cultivate before your life-force can be more successfully activated. It is perhaps no coincidence that the enigmatic figure Thoth (also referred to as Mercury your ruler, and Hermes) is analogous of your dynamic astrological background. Human ascension was aided greatly through his inscribing's of all knowledge and wisdom on the famed 'Emerald Tablets', and you can learn much from your planet's links with this profound universally accessible wisdom. The dynamic Archer's spirit already embodies the philosophies contained within the hermetic teachings, but the Twins need a little more help to tap into this magic, for the meanings can only be found in further depths than you have perhaps ever ventured. Once you hit your stride, however, you will see that there is no turning back to the simplistic, surface-skimming, superficial ways of thinking that used to be your way of life.

WHAT THE ARCHER CAN ULTIMATELY TEACH THE TWINS

Release ★ Superficiality of character, restlessness, flightiness, boredom, indiscriminate information-gathering, dispersion, double-dealing, pretence, trickery, the conflict between commitment and freedom, empty gossip, superficial social interactions, lack of depth, living too much in the moment, the need for instant gratification, taking the easy path.

Embrace ★ Broad-mindedness, philosophical outlook, vision, nobility, truth, generous feelings, authenticity, stronger convictions and belief systems, discerning information-gathering, higher education, commitment *and* freedom, more meaningful social interactions, considering the future, reflection, considering all options before deciding on one path.

To evolve to your fullest potential, Sagittarius teaches you to embrace whatever higher power or personal truth you believe in with more commitment; to seek and *live* the deeper meaning of life; to be less fickle and superficial and to delve a bit deeper into your life's true meaning; to search for enriching experiences; to not take everything at face value; to take a more enduring, sustained approach; to be more far-sighted rather than simply living each day as it comes; to question things; to embrace a more profound curiosity that probes *underneath* the surface.

Overall, Sagittarius has a more dynamic expression than Gemini's basic, simplistic way of communicating, and can teach you how to increase your effectiveness in this domain. He will illuminate you with his dazzling, high-minded wit. You are flighty, quick as a flash and nervous; Sagittarius is not - he will ponder a question or idea for as long as it takes. And that is the fundamental difference between you two. Feel inspired by the Sagittarian's links to the higher planes, and he may even respond by allowing you insights into his brilliant mind and take you under his wing if you will let him. And you may even find that the higher you soar and the wider the landscape below becomes, that the grass is indeed green *everywhere*.

MAGIC, DRAWING, ATTRACTION, SPELLS, RITUALS, WISHING & POWER

A Note on the Universe

Within each of us resides the merging of the Sun and the Moon, the dance of the constellations, the vibrations of the planets, and the vast microcosm and macrocosm of the entire *Universe*. Uni means 'one' and Verse means 'song'; therefore, the word Universe literally means 'One Song'. If you learn to tune yourself in, you can even hear it!

What is Magic?

Magic is a kind of special energy that is beyond description, and like most kinds of energy it has its own rules and ways of being manipulated. It remains an elusive term, and no definition has ever really found Universal acceptance. Attempts to separate it from superstition, religion and other-worldly phenomena on the one hand, and 'science' on the other, are ridden with difficulties. However slippery the term 'magic' might be, there is a general agreement that most of us wish for more of its presence in our lives and often fall short of achieving this wish.

Those performing spells, 'asking the Universe', wishing, praying, or undertaking rituals, are using this very special energy to draw things to them. Learning to manipulate energy in these ways is never hard (and shouldn't be), but it can be complex and does require knowledge, practice, creativity, patience and above all, imagination. Most of us use simple magic every day, whether by saying little prayers, making wishes, visualising, and exchanging - sending out and receiving - good, positive or hopeful vibes. When you understand that all the forces and magic you need are *within* you, and you learn to *believe* in that power, you are then able to make all manner of changes to your life and, most importantly, yourself.

Magic is an invisible force which connects and permeates everything. Every thought you have and every action you take, will affect the strength of this force, and can be influenced and directed towards a specific purpose by using certain means. The most important of these are your intentions, facing in the direction of your desired outcome, your will and your *belief* that it works. The more you want something to happen, and the clearer you can visualise the desired outcome, the stronger your will and feelings towards it will be, ensuring an avalanche of amazing people, events and circumstances will flow into your experiences, gathering speed, momentum and power as it nears your goal or dream.

The Universe (or whichever higher power you believe in) works for us and through us. Ideas are given to us but they must be carried out *through* us, in the form of asking or acting or performing a ritual or casting a specific spell. The Universe's abundance is your abundance, and it flows through your mind into manifestation. The Universe or Divine Being in which you believe, gives you the necessary ideas and clothes them with all that is needed to bring them into form when we ask *believing*.

Based on ancient human beliefs, systems and superstitions, declaring what you want and acting out your deepest desires can actually help to make things happen. Magical ideas include the notion that thought affects matter and that the trained imagination can alter the physical world, that all aspects of the Universe are interdependent and that we can discover connections and correspondences between everyday occurrences and cosmic, or Divine, energies. A miracle or a wish coming true can suggest something is going on that extends beyond the laws of nature, that something unseen has occurred; but just because we cannot see it or touch it, it doesn't mean it's not there. Magic exists, especially if you truly believe it does, but science is so far incapable of capturing its essence or the rationale behind it. Personally, I prefer to leave that task to the higher powers of the Universe.

To help your dreams come true and to use your inborn power to its full effect, you can employ boosters based on the special energies and qualities of your Sun sign. These 'boosters' are chosen to be in alignment with the purpose of a particular goal, and contain energies of their own which will enhance the strength of your spell, prayer, ritual or 'asking'. Specific magical energies can be invoked by carrying out a spell or ceremony using specific herbs or colours, or on a particular day of the week, according to either your Sun sign (to heighten the power of the asking), and/or that is in sympathy with that for which you are asking (I have included days of the week for other Sun signs and spell types).

Some materials and boosters you can use to increase the power, magic or energy in any area of your life include: candles, wish lists (written on an appropriate piece of paper written with a specially-chosen writing tool), symbols, affirmations, chants, incense, herbs and flowers, locations, colours, days of the week, elements, crystals and gemstones, animal symbols, charms, talismans, amulets, gods and goddesses, essential oils, planetary hours and your Solar totem animals. All are covered, some more briefly than others, for your very special Sun sign to radiate the energy to powerfully draw your wildest dreams towards you!

Overall, it pays to remember that the Universe (or whatever higher power/s or force/s you happen to believe in) creates *through* you that to which you give your attention. What you contemplate becomes the law of your being, and through your pure unwavering belief, is eventually brought through to manifestation on the material plane. What you think about is entirely up to you. But just be mindful that whatever you think about the most becomes your dominant thought, then your main point of attraction, and is ultimately magnified until it becomes your reality or your experience. So choose your thoughts with care. And to quote Ralph Waldo Emerson, "Be careful what you set your heart upon, for it will surely be yours." I carry a copy of this beautiful prophecy in my purse as its words resonate so strongly with me. In other words, be mindful about what you're wishing for, for you will most probably get it, whether it's good or bad - magic, after all, doesn't discriminate. Just make your dominant thoughts good ones, and you will attract everything you set your heart and intentions upon. Good luck!!

ASTROLOGY & MAGIC

"Everyone practices magic, whether they realise it or not, for magic is the art of attracting particular influences, events and situations within human life. Magic is a natural phenomenon because the Universe is reflexive, responding to human thoughts, aspirations and desires ..."
David Fideler, *Jesus Christ, Sun of God*

Astrology is the most sublime of the occult * sciences, while at the same time it is one of the most practical for everyday application, for it divines the human soul itself. The cosmos, particularly the patterns that formed across it at the exact moment we were born, indicates the road along which our mental and spiritual endowments are likely to impel us, therefore enabling us to prepare in advance for life's battles, pitfalls, milestones, celebrations and of course to make the utmost of opportunities. Such is the magic of the human mind, that it can 'see' into the future and relive the past without having to be physically present in either, and when combined with astrological *knowing*, particularly the knowing that springs from understanding some of the dynamics of our natal chart, however basic, our inner - and outer - magic can be lifted to phenomenal heights.

In ancient times, not only was astrology the ardent study of the most learned and powerful minds, but among the masses of ordinary people its authority and guidance was accepted and followed without question. How this powerful knowledge was used was - and still is - up to the individual, but all who used it applied it to their perceived advantage.

As primitive humans observed the skies, no doubt they gradually realised that certain stars upon which their fate depended accompanied the seasons, or certain times of the year. They may also have reasoned that if governed their fate, they also governed their bodies, and it is therefore conceivable that the skies were associated with Divine influence. Certain celestial influences were believed to emanate from the thirty-six decans of the signs, and the mysterious but apparent effect that they exercised upon humans were thought to be due to a subtle ether shed by the heavenly stars and spheres on the Earth, that affected not only people, but also other animals, plants and minerals. For the ancient mind, linking magic with astrology may have also provided a much needed sense of predictability and patterns.

Early astrologers named and made associations with the imaginary divisions of the twelve signs and the twelve houses, and people born under a certain sign were said to inherit to an extent, its properties and nature. They also believed that the influence of the planets and stars corresponded with the medicinal properties of certain plants and minerals. They therefore asserted that the influence of a star or planetary position would affect the type of medicine or healing they would offer a subject to attain the most beneficial outcome. Throughout the writings of early philosophers and theorists, there is constant reference to this unmistakable mystic connection between the seven known planets and Earthly affairs and ailments. The seven metals were connected with the seven planets, to which the seven colours and the seven transformations were added. So the alchemist came to share the astrological doctrine that each planet ruled some mineral: The Sun ruled gold, the Moon silver, Mars iron, Venus copper, Saturn lead, Jupiter tin, and Mercury quicksilver. Consequently, in alchemical symbolism the same sign came to represent the metal and its corresponding planet.

In subsequent years, astrology became closely related to alchemical knowledge and development, and the alchemist came to be regarded as an authority not only on the transmutation of metals, but also on astrology and magic. This goes some of the way to explaining how magic and divination, which had always been inseparably bound up with astrology, came to be associated with alchemy. In all the occult sciences, the supreme power was believed to be in the stars above, and from their mysterious emanations all the metals, crystals, minerals, plants and herbs derived their special properties over time. Further, as alchemy became ever more spiritual and concerned with more abstract and philosophical concepts, eventually it was considered that the transmutation of lead into gold was simply a metaphor for the transformation of base matter, in this case the human soul, into a much purer and higher state of wisdom and being.

The Sun and Moon were believed to have greater influence over the human body than all the other heavenly bodies, and to exert their influence in various ways whenever they entered a certain sign of the zodiac. And although the Moon was traditionally regarded as the most important factor of a horoscope, the Sun has come into its own in later centuries, with the result that almost everyone knows their Sun sign but only those who have delved deeper are aware of the sign their natal Moon falls in. For this reason, I have chosen to focus this book series on the twelve Sun signs, as this is what the majority of people are most familiar with.

The following pages contain methods, energies, materials and objects which may be used to increase the magic and power of your Sun sign's influence upon you. Precious stones, flowers, colours and so on, are regarded as having a potent effect upon good fortune by attuning your mind to receive harmonious vibrations from the astral forces that surround you.

Finally, a basic working knowledge of basic astronomy and astrology is an asset when working with luck, abundance, wealth and personal power. You can attract more of these things when you align yourself with the workings of the wider Universe, the movement of the Sun, stars, Moon and planets and become aware of the correlations between the outer cycles of the skies and the inner cycles within yourself. Also, for those who are knowledgeable about Moon phases, equinoxes and solstices, a world of lucky possibilities can also magically open up to you. You don't need to know about astrology's deepest complexities to understand how everything interrelates; just learning the basics will give you an edge - and hopefully the following lucky tips will provide you with at least a small glimpse into the insights gleaned from your Sun sign, which I am certain will endow upon you the potential for amazing results to manifest in your life - and maybe even a step up one further rung towards the heavens!

* The word 'occult' comes from the Latin *occultus*, which literally means 'knowledge of the hidden'.

USING COLOURS, CRYSTALS, DEITIES, PLANTS, FOODS & MATERIAL SUBSTANCES FOR INCREASING POWER & MAGNETISING MAGIC

Alchemist, reformer and mystic Henry Cornelius Agrippa, born in 1486, in his principal work, *On Occult Philosophy*, expressed his belief in the doctrines of astrology and in the theory that the spirit of the world exists in the body of the world, just as the human spirit exists in the body of man. He contended that this spirit also abounds in the celestial bodies and descends in the rays of stars, so that the things influenced by their rays become conformable to them. By this spirit every occult property is conveyed into metals, stones, herbs and animals, through the Sun, Moon and planets, and even through the stars beyond and higher than the planets. A firm believer in the efficacy of charms, he stated that they may "be worn on the body bound to any part of it or hung around the neck, changing sickness into health or health into sickness." I believe the same effect could be applied to wishing and the thinking of positive thoughts, to mean, "Changing thoughts and dreams into manifest reality." He also recommended that these charms be worn in the form of finger rings (that have been created using the materials in agreement and harmony with your Sun Sign's magical energy).

Material substances are connected with abstract purposes by a complex but highly usable and accessible system of correspondences. Use these time-honoured connections in your own spells and wishes to magnetise your desires to you. The following pages will give you some materials, energies, forces and ideas you can summon the power of in order to enhance your magic and luck.

PLANETS

The Planetary influence of the day is important when 'asking' for something. If you are wishing for luck, for example, try working with your Sun sign's inherent energies combined with the perfect day of the week for it. So a Geminian might try using his natural intellect and articulate expression, to ask for greater luck on a Thursday, which is Jupiter's Day and Jupiter is renowned for being a lucky planet, or better still, ask for luck on a Wednesday, which is Mercury's Day, planetary ruler of Gemini, at the time of day when Jupiter's influence is at its most powerful (information about planetary hours for each day of the week can be found on the Internet or in books on the subject, and can be complex and detailed. It is an art to memorise the correct times, days and energies for the correct spells. If you are determined enough to achieve your dream or goal however, you will be determined enough to put in the research to do it properly!) Here is a very simplified list of the days of the week and their meanings:

DAYS OF THE WEEK & THEIR POWERS

MONDAY ★ Moon
Cancer

The Divine feminine, changes, intuition, emotions, secrets, dealing with women, purity, goodness, perfection, unity, psychic ability, magic, spirituality, invoking a goddess's or angel's guidance, anything that fluctuates, contracts, increases or decreases.

TUESDAY ★ Mars
Aries & Scorpio

Enthusiasm, competition, passion, energy, courage, protection, victory, anything requiring assertiveness, standing up for yourself, or a 'fighting spirit', determination, vitality, sexuality, self-confidence, men's power, men's mysteries, drive, ambition, achievement, triumph, masculinity.

WEDNESDAY ★ Mercury
Gemini & Virgo

Education, travel, exams, study, communication,

making connections, thinking, dealing with siblings, writing and speaking, knowledge, learning, adaptability, charm, youth, absorbing information.

THURSDAY ★ Jupiter
Sagittarius & Pisces

Increase and expansion of anything (remember to be careful what you wish for), luck, growth, influence, worldly power, accomplishment, fulfilment, gambling, philosophy, higher education, abundance, optimism.

FRIDAY ★ Venus
Taurus & Libra

Love, luxury, the arts, indulgence, beauty, marriage, money, prosperity, fertility, women's power, women's mysteries, grace, charm, appeal, hope, pleasure, decorating, self-worth, self-esteem, personal values, business partnerships, romance, creativity, sharing, bonding.

SATURDAY ★ Saturn
Capricorn & Aquarius

Long-term goals, career, institutions, establishments, security, investments, karma, reversal, structure, protection, solitude, privacy, determination, ending, blocking, renewing, transforming, anything to do with the public.

SUNDAY ★ Sun
Leo

All-purpose, success, wishes, generosity, happiness, optimism, spirit/essence, recognition, health, vitality, material wealth, invoking a god's aid or guidance, personal empowerment, spirituality, the Divine masculine.

YOUR NATAL MOON PHASE

Although this book is aimed at enhancing your life through the energy of your Sun sign, a bit of Lunar help can give your wishing a boost! As well as using the planetary days and hours system to add a bit of zest to your wish fulfilment, try combining your Sun sign's power periods with your natal Moon phase (your natal Moon phase can be calculated using a number of sources on the internet, or through an astrologer), or even studying which constellation the Moon is situated in at certain times, to increase the power of your spells and asking rituals. For example, you might like to 'ask' for a promotion at work during a New/Waxing Moon period, particularly if the Moon happens to fall under an auspicious sign for career advancement, such as Capricorn. Your natal Moon phase can also be used to similar effect, by researching when your Moon phase will coincide with a certain Lunar constellation position.

In most astrological interpretations the Sun is regarded as the most important, central feature of a natal chart. But to many the Moon is equally, if not more, important than the Sun sign. Many ancient cultures considered the Moon sign to be more significant. The Moon passes through the 12 signs about every 2.5 days, usually covering the whole zodiac in around 27.3 days. The Moon symbolises our inner world, the world of feeling, emotions, habitual responses, instincts, intuition, security and the subconscious. It describes our nurturing style and needs, our emotional response to life, our attitudes and likely reactions to others, our instinctive and habitual responses, the receptive feminine side of ourselves, our experience of our mother or mother figure, and our childhood experience. It represents the soul. In relationships it symbolises how we like to be nurtured and cared for, and the potential depth of our involvement on personal intimate levels.

For many centuries, people across the world have recognised that the Moon influences the affairs of all living things on planet Earth. The waxing Moon appears to have a drawing, increasing and enhancing effect, whereas the waning Moon has a decreasing, receding and withdrawing effect. All things that come into being are stamped with the qualities of the prevailing Moon stage. It seems that people born during certain Lunar phases tend to share specific attributes with other people born during this same phase. In turn, their attributes will be subtly different from those of individuals born during any of the other stages in the Moon cycle. Knowing exactly which phase of the Moon you were born under gives you all kinds of extraordinarily valuable insights into your character, emotions, behaviour and motivations in life. It can make you aware of your deepest underlying drives, the fundamental purpose that you are drawn towards in life and the contribution you can make to others and society during the course of your lifetime. This knowledge may enable you to intuit and make the most of your own personal cyclical pattern that you go through each month, and allow you to know when the most auspicious periods of time are for you and your affairs, nurture yourself and channel your energies in the most positive directions.

Because this Lunar pattern repeats itself every month, you will find that you can even pace yourself on a long-term basis. This will enable you to effectively target your efforts and goals on periods of time that you know will be potentially fortunate for you. You may in fact find that your birth phase corresponds with the days of the month when you have abundant energy, feel inspired and can generate new ideas with ease. During this period, you should work towards the fruition of your efforts, bring your dreams into light and reach for the stars!

The Lunar Phases Are:

★ New Moon
★ First/Waxing Crescent
★ First Quarter
★ Waxing Gibbous Moon
★ Full Moon
★ Waning Gibbous / Disseminating Moon
★ Last Quarter
★ Waning Crescent / Balsamic Moon
★ Back to the New Moon

SPELLS, MAGIC & WISHING WITH MOON PHASES

Though the Moon has eight astronomical phases, it is the three phases corresponding to maiden, mother and crone that are the most significant in spells, ritual, wish magic and psychic work. By tuning into the physical Moon we can understand and harness these distinct energy phases in our daily lives and magical worlds. The four primary Lunar phases are the New Moon, First Quarter, Full Moon and the Last Quarter. Depending on what sort of spell you wish to perform, your spell should take place during one of these cycles or time periods. Each phase of the Moon is good for some types of magic, but not so much for others.

NEW MOON, WAXING & FIRST QUARTER

In astronomical terms, the New Moon occurs when the Moon rises and sets at the same time as the Sun. Both bodies are found in the same position compared with the Earth. Therefore, a Solar eclipse can only ever occur at the New Moon, when the two luminaries are found, for a short time, in a perfect line relative to the Earth, with the Moon positioned between the Sun and the Earth. The New Moon's sunlit face is hidden from the Earth.

In astrological terms, the New Moon occurs at a time when the Sun and the Moon are found in the same degree of the zodiac and therefore occupy the same zodiac sign, forming a conjunction, or a 'fusing' of energies.

In astronomical terms, the First Quarter occurs seven days after the New Moon. Seen from the Earth, this phase makes the Moon like a crescent, forming the shape of a capital D.

In astrological terms, it occurs when the Sun and the Moon form a ninety-degree angle, or the square aspect, inside the zodiac, the Moon always preceding the Sun.

As the New Moon marks the beginning of a new cycle, it symbolises fresh starts. This is an exceptional time to work magic and make wishes for new beginnings, and for the conception and initiation of new projects. Use this Moon phase for improving health, the gradual increase of prosperity, attracting good luck, fertility magic, finding new love, friendship or romance, job hunting, making plans for the future and increasing your general spiritual or psychic awareness.

Overall, the Waxing Crescent and First Quarter Moon phases are appropriate for spells, rituals and workings that involve growth, healing and increase. This is a period of time lasting approximately two weeks, to draw things toward you and increase things, such as love, prosperity and new opportunities. During this period is the time to bless new projects, anything that requires energy to grow, such as gardens, business ventures, new homes, or educational pursuits. Personal growth and healing are accented, as is 'attraction magic' - drawing something to you such as love, abundance, health, success or a new path - and if done well, you can expect results by the next Full Moon. Magical workings for gain, increase or bringing things to you should be initiated when the Moon is waxing (or New, going from Dark to Full). A time for divination of all kinds, spells of spiritual intention, and for any creative project you wish to see birthed, with magical and fruitful results.

While making a wish within the first forty-eight hours after the New Moon is a powerful way of helping it come to fruition, the most potent time for making wishes is actually within the first eight hours of the exact time of its position. Write down your wish list within this first eight hours on a piece of appropriately coloured paper with a special writing tool, and be sure to capture the essence of your wish by wording it in a way that charges your emotions and simply feels 'right'. Make a maximum of ten wishes (less is perfectly fine too), as making too many wishes might disperse their energy too much to be effective. After writing down your list and releasing your wishes to the Universe in whichever form you feel happy with, keep your list and check on it in a few days', weeks' or months' time to assess whether anything has shifted in the direction of your listed dreams, desires or goals. I'll bet it has - or at the very least, something even better has arrived in its place!

Although the first forty-eight hours after the New Moon is the most potent time to make a special wish, you can begin Waxing Moon magic when you can see the crescent in the sky and continue until the day before the Full Moon. The closer to the Full Moon, the more intense the energies. In fact, a personally devised ritual using any special Lunar-associated materials over three days up to and including the Full Moon is excellent for something you require urgently or within a short timeframe.

In some cultures, people turn over silver coins or jewellery three times when the crescent Moon appears in the sky and make a wish. As the Moon grows, it is believed that prosperity and good fortune will grow too.

While the New Moon is not known as a time for 'banishing' or releasing things we no longer want in our lives, I feel that if we are to ask and wish for things, we need to make room to receive them. Making room means that the Universe can slot it right into our lives where we have cleared our paths for it. Clutter, unwanted things, unhappy relationships, possessions that no longer serve us, are all things we can banish. So, to help what you are asking for come into your life quicker, the New Moon is a particularly opportune time to throw a few things out so you can make way for the new and clear up some space for that which you are wishing for. What are you waiting for? Start creating a space for your wishes today!

FULL MOON

In astronomical terms, the Full Moon occurs 14 days after the New Moon, on the day when the Moon sets at the same time the Sun rises, or conversely. The two luminaries are effectively facing each other, with the Earth in between, the Sun shining its light onto the reflective Moon, giving it the fully lit up appearance of a giant, bright, perfectly round sphere. Indeed, its entire face is bathed in sunlight. A Lunar eclipse can only occur at the Full Moon, when the Sun, Moon and Earth are all in line, and the Earth hides the lit side of the Moon to us.

In astrological terms, a Full Moon occurs at the time when the Sun and Moon are 180 degrees apart inside the zodiac, and therefore positioned in opposite signs, forming an opposition aspect.

The highest energy occurs at the Full Moon, making this is a powerful time for all manner of magical workings. Use the Full Moon phase for any immediate need, a sudden boost of power or courage, psychic protection, a change of career or location, travel, healing acute health conditions, the consummation of love or a commitment, justice, ambition and promotion of all kinds. This phase lasts approximately 3 days - 24 hours before the exact Full Moon, the day of, and 24 hours after it, according to many sources - giving us 3 full days to perform our spells. However, we are not strictly limited to a three-day period; the power of this phase can actually be accessed for seven days - three days prior to, the night of, and the three days after the Full Moon. The Full Moon period is when the Moon is at her most powerful, being the most luminous and radiant part of the cycle. Known as the 'high tide' of psychic power, the Full Moon represents culmination, climax, fulfilment and abundance. The Full Moon governs all kinds of magic, including manifestation, banishing, and is particularly good for calling forth protection and heightening your intuitive abilities. The Full Moon contains magic that calls forth personal power, fertility, spiritual development, and psychic awareness. Cleansing of ritual tools, crystals, wish lists, Tarot decks, and the like can be done during this phase. Magic worked during the Full Moon often takes one complete cycle to come to fruition. Try also reaffirming your desires during the New Moon to give them an added nudge in the right direction.

LAST QUARTER OR WANING MOON

In astronomical terms, the Last Quarter, or Waning Moon, occurs twenty-one days after the New Moon. The time difference between the rising and setting of the two luminaries is reduced to what it was at the First Quarter. Viewed from the Earth, the Moon resembles a crescent whose lit up area is decreasing in size, forming the shape of a capital C.

In astrological terms, the Waning Moon occurs when the Sun and Moon are positioned at ninety degree angles of each other in the zodiac, forming the square aspect again. However, during this phase, the Sun is instead *ahead* of the Moon.

The Waning Moon represents the Lunar cycle from Full to Dark. Any spells and magic performed during this period is based purely around banishing and releasing. It could involve releasing things which no longer serve you (such as behaviours, material things, relationships and attitudes), banishing negative energies, and removing obstacles which are standing in the way of achieving your goals or dreams. The Waning Moon is the best time for cleansing, gently releasing, eliminating, expelling and completion. It is of great assistance when you are wanting to let go of something, or someone, gradually. The Dark of the Moon, the period when the Moon is no longer visible to the naked eye, until the New Moon, is the most useful time for divination of all kinds.

★ What is your natal Moon phase type?
Can you think of ways you can combine it with the power of your Sun sign to effect change and bring about wonderful happenings? ★

HARNESSING YOUR PERSONAL MOON MAGIC ★ MOON IN GEMINI

When the Moon is in your sign of Gemini, it is a great time for working magic around: Multi-tasking, intellect, awareness, agility, adaptability and flexibility. Suggested operations could be around rituals and spells to learn to cultivate greater energy, vitality, and liveliness, to attract more social invitations, and for any type of learning, study, communication or research. It is also an opportune time to tap into finishing the old and beginning the new and fresh, for revitalising your friendships and relationships, and for helping you juggle everything and keep all your balls in the air at once. With the Moon in Gemini, the mental arts are emphasised, so anything intellectually-based such as study, enrolling in a short course, and exchanging information with other like-minded people such as through an internet chat room or book group, would be ideal to begin or undertake at this time.

THE MOON ★ WHAT IT REPRESENTS IN THE HUMAN PSYCHE & NATAL CHART

The Moon in the sky shines with the reflected light of the Sun. Although not a planet, the Moon is our nearest celestial neighbour and exerts a great influence upon us. The gravitational pull of the Moon affects our body fluids, which contribute to about 90 per cent of our biological make-up. It moves at approximately half a degree per hour and takes an average of 27.3 days to pass through all twelve zodiac signs, staying in each for around 2.5 days.

In astrology the Moon corresponds with the way in which we reflect and respond to what is going on around us. It has to do with our feelings, emotions and instincts and, in the same way the Moon influences the tides on planet Earth, it symbolises the ebb and flow of our emotional nature, our moods, fluctuations and changeability. The Moon is the archetype of the Mother, which is within us all, and represents the primary feminine principle in the natal chart. It is through the Moon that we express our parental instincts - caring, nurturing, protecting, and sensitivity. The Moon has links with the past and the subconscious and it is from this almost primitive source that our natural instinctual forces flow.

The Moon is essentially a feminine principle and associates with the inner personality, receptivity, passivity and inward-oriented feelings. It can act as an inner guide to the deeper self, the unconscious self, figures half-shrouded in mystery, linking the hidden personal world of the subconscious to the clearer world of personal awareness.

The Moon is the innermost core of our being, private feelings, habitual reactions and subconscious habits. It is the caring, nurturing sustainer of life, the 'mother' of the zodiac. It tells us about how we seek security, our urge to nurture, our nurturing style, our responses and feelings and moods. The innermost core of our being, private feelings, subconscious habits. It is concerned with habits, mothering, habitual/instinctive responses and personality. It is our karma, our soul, our past.

The Moon represents our mother or mother figure, our feminine side, maternal instinct, our nurturing style and needs, our unconscious self, our emotional reactions, the subconscious, our feelings, instincts, intuition, receptivity, habits, what we need to feel secure, fluctuations, cycles, moods, and our childhood. Its position in the birth chart is very significant, because as well as revealing feminine qualities and the potential gentleness and tenderness of a being, the Moon also reveals important information about the experiences and expression of the five senses.

The Moon is essentially receptive and passive; it reflects the life experience rather than initiating it. Fluctuating and cyclical, the Moon is the planet (although technically a satellite) of the childhood experience, and instinctual reactions. It represents the mother (a child's experience and expectations of their mother), maternal instincts and the feminine principle, indicating how strongly these manifest in an individual, male or female.

As it represents what our childhood experience is likely to be, and childhood is essentially a time where our consciousness has not yet fully developed, our Moon sign traits seem to be more apparent in our younger years. We will usually show our Moon sign traits more so than our Sun sign traits during this developing period of infancy and early childhood, until we have the presence of mind to more consciously develop our ego and true core Self (the Sun).

The symbol for the Moon ☽ is a representation of its crescent in its waxing phase from new to full, but it can also be seen as two half circles - these form a bowl shape, a receptacle, a feminine container that 'receives' and 'holds' anything put into it. The half circle, unlike the full circle of the Sun, is finite and incomplete, almost as if striving for wholeness.

The Moon represents our soul.

YOUR MOON SIGN

The Sun / Moon Polarity
Conscious & Unconscious, Night & Day, Yin & Yang

"Man does, woman is."
Edward Edinger

Your Moon Sign, representing your soul, and your Sun sign, representing your spirit, work together to form the foundation of your basic personality, expression and nature. If you know what your Moon sign is, look it up below and read how it works with your Geminian Sun to blend your mind, soul and spirit.

♈ **With the Moon in ARIES, Sun in Gemini**, you are likely to be ★ Effervescent, observant, fresh, decisive, astute, self-interested, superficial, egocentric, alert, light-hearted, emotionally detached, impatient with lesser minds, zestful, intolerant of idleness, independent, adventurous, flighty, temperamental, nimble, monopolising of conversations, inconsistent, vital, fun-loving, unreliable, on the go, busy, insensitive, self-reliant, energetic, dextrous, persuasive, emotionally bold and reckless, restless, speak before thinking, active, a fast communicator, intellectual, inventive, insensitive to feelings of others, ideas-oriented, lively, witty, frank, bright, charming, inspired, humorous, flirty, spontaneous, sociable, popular, conversational, clear-thinking, sparkling, and in possession of an enviable gift of the gab.

Sun/Moon Harmony Rating ★ *8 out of 10*

♉ **With the Moon in TAURUS, Sun in Gemini**, you are likely to be ★ Pragmatically intellectual, stubborn, materialistic, sensually flirtatious, superficial, conflicted between security and freedom, entrepreneurial, able to turn ideas into realities, flexible without compromising self, able to offer practical support and generosity to others, easily tempted by pleasures, tenacious, socially engaging, logical and detached in emotional matters, able to apply your intelligence, friendly but flighty, capable, determined, resourceful, ambitious, torn between quiet and activity, persistent, resistant to spiritual matters, and dedicated to grounding your inspiration and enthusiasm so they are more workable.

Sun/Moon Harmony Rating ★ *5.5 out of 10*

♊ **With the Moon in GEMINI, Sun in Gemini**, you are likely to be ★ A free spirit, lively, superficial, mentally agile, suave, talented, expressive, a jack-of-all-trades, changeable, frivolous, friendly, bright, breezy, adaptable, shallow, emotionally versatile, quick-witted, cerebral, flippant, perceptive, a mimic and a juggler, nervous, on the go, clever, inspiring, stimulating, sociable, detached, flexible, curious, emotionally impulsive, restless, gossipy, easily bored, objective, communicative, unsentimental, emotionally naïve, childlike, gifted, a wonderful friend, popular, funny, charming, witty, open towards and perceptive of new ideas, intellectual, squandering of your natural talents, reluctant to face the darker aspects of life, too busy to deal with feelings, and ruled by your mind rather than your heart.

Sun/Moon Harmony Rating ★ *8 out of 10*

♋ **With the Moon in CANCER, Sun in Gemini,** you are likely to be ★ Intellectually intuitive, emotionally expressive, changeable, moody, nervous, versatile, never content, imaginative, poetic, intelligently kind, helpful, companionable, emotionally lofty, idealistic, impressionable, receptive, cleverly self-expressive, shrewd, emotionally defensive, unstable, able to express insights on a personal level, self-protective, innately interested in others yet private, self-preserving, devoted to family and siblings, dedicated to neighbourhood social events and causes, clannish, perceptive, and occasionally moved to emotional evasiveness.

Sun/Moon Harmony Rating ★ *6 out of 10*

♌ **With the Moon in LEO, Sun in Gemini,** you are likely to be ★ Proud, independent, individualistic, flighty on the surface with a great strength within, positive, a good dramatist and story-teller, improvising, fearless, sociable, generous, passionate, radiant, popular, spirited, inspirational, contagiously optimistic, youthful, enthusiastic, romantic, open, flexible, witty, a natural salesperson, demonstrative, charismatic, extroverted, honest, warm, bold, inclined to get carried away, direct, vain, frivolous, lively, friendly, expressive, ambitious, self-centred, boastful, emotionally idealistic, helpful, intelligent, a colourful conservationist, warmly convivial, and in possession of a childlike sense of fun.

Sun/Moon Harmony Rating ★ 8 out of 10

♍ **With the Moon in VIRGO, Sun in Gemini,** you are likely to be ★ Intelligent, judgemental, cool, calm and collected, critical, verbally expressive, a worrier, clever, discriminating, logical, awkward about showing feelings, analytical, technically skilled, a perfectionist, methodical, studious, innovative, mentally alert, a good communicator, efficient, aspiring, busy, mentally dextrous, efficient, undemonstrative, objectively rational, cool-headed, altruistic, bright, quick-witted, sociable yet uptight, and in possession of an overly active mind that can't switch off.

Sun/Moon Harmony Rating ★ 6 out of 10

♎ **With the Moon in LIBRA, Sun in Gemini,** you are likely to be ★ Lively, intellectual, sociable, gregarious, friendly, easygoing, sporadically affectionate, popular, a hider of feelings, verbally expressive, charming, approachable, popular, distanced from your true emotional power, accessible, civilised, cooperative, approval-seeking, hospitable, indecisive, interested in people, romantically idealistic, flirtatious, acutely observant, quick-witted, persuasive, artistically sensitive, abstract, emotionally naïve, and conflicted between independence and needing social sustenance through partnerships.

Sun/Moon Harmony Rating ★ *8.5 out of 10* **

♏ **With the Moon in SCORPIO, Sun in Gemini,** you are likely to be ★ Intensely expressive, provocative, powerfully intellectual, a great social force, magnetic, socially persuasive, multifaceted, highly charged, restless, extreme, keenly insightful, acutely perceptive, investigative, intriguingly popular, resourceful, vitally sensual, alternating between breezy and intense, penetrative yet surface-skimming, sarcastic, scathing, passionate yet dispassionate, courageous, an astute observer, quick-witted, deep-hearted, colourful, independent, charismatic, communicative yet secretive, self-reliant, potentially ruthless and manipulative, and socially influential.

Sun/Moon Harmony Rating ★ *6 out of 10*

♐ **With the Moon in SAGITTARIUS, Sun in Gemini,** you are likely to be ★ Eager, curious, seeking, open to experience, emotionally immature but responsive, adventurous, friendly, independent, idealistic, a traveller of body and mind, sociable, honest, insincere, an eternal student, a traveller, rationalising, impatient with petty details and restrictions of daily life, flamboyant, generous, in possession of a voracious appetite for people and experiences, full of good ideas, intellectually insightful, indiscreet, a great talker, prone to preach, blunt, intellectual, inquisitive, an adventurer, freedom-seeking, distant from your feelings, emotionally reckless, a free spirit, non-committal, a good teacher, in possession of an intelligent sense of humour, far-sighted, intellectually speedy, optimistic, a lover of learning, inspiring, outrageous, spontaneous, aspiring, gregarious, expansive, verbose, superficially philosophical, a voyager, and guided by reason rather than emotion.

Sun/Moon Harmony Rating ★ *9 out of 10*

♑ **With the Moon in CAPRICORN, Sun in Gemini,** you are likely to be ★ Steadfast, resourceful, witty, independent, a devoted friend, striving, driven to succeed, cool, a cynical optimist, unemotional, intellectually wise, shrewd, clever, attracted to social events with an intellectual slant, impatient with the emotional realm, bright, organised, efficient, understanding of practical applications and wisdom, a realist, a clear-thinker, inventive, socially honourable, fearless, uptight, socially rigid, self-contained, aware of human character, sardonically humorous, serious yet carefree, and sociable yet solitary.

Sun/Moon Harmony Rating ★ *7 out of 10*

♒ **With the Moon in AQUARIUS, Sun in Gemini,** you are likely to be ★ Gregarious, unconventional, witty, in possession of a unique sense of humour, prophetic, clear-thinking, restless, tolerant, independent, idealistic, alert, adaptable, neglectful of realities, emotionally detached, eccentric, 'different', paradoxical, honest, flighty, nervous, original, forward-moving, inventive, impersonal in relationships, clear-headed, highly observant, acutely aware of the human condition, progressive, scientifically oriented, objective, living an unusual lifestyle in some way, well-meaning, open to the unusual, emotionally naïve, freedom-loving, unorthodox, impractical, humanitarian, committed to your ideals and convictions, and in possession of an insatiable sociable streak.

Sun/Moon Harmony Rating ★ 8 out of 10 **

♓ **With the Moon in PISCES, Sun in Gemini,** you are likely to be ★ Whimsical, childlike, versatile, changeable, imaginative, intuitive, able to blend realism with mysticism, idealistic, unable to concentrate, cheeky, lacking in boundaries, confused, good-natured, friendly, emotionally intelligent, apt to wander off and go into flights of fancy, hot and cold emotions, sentimental, independent but vulnerable, an intellectual poet, humorous, intelligently insightful, generous, receptive, creative, reverent, forgiving, superficial, adaptable, prone to drifting and wasting time in daydreams, impressionable, idealistic but easily swayed, gullible, impractical, evasive, perceptive, chameleon-like, moody, vacillating, talkative, nervous, submissive yet cunning, emotionally intelligent, able to mix and work with all types of people, and aware of the needs of others.

Sun/Moon Harmony Rating ★ *8 out of 10*

YOUR BODY & HEALTH

"A physician without a knowledge of astrology has no right to call himself a physician."
Hippocrates (born c. 460 BC)

Hippocrates, the fifth century BC Greek physician and 'father of medicine' and supposed author of the Hippocratic Oath, maintained that no one should be allowed to practise medicine who had not first studied astrology. Another Greek physician, Claudius Galen, brought together a huge range of knowledge and ideas in the second century AD which dominated medical practice until the 17th century. Among his teachings was a diagnostic technique which assumed that illnesses and their treatments were affected by and governed by the phases of the Moon. For centuries, astrology was a compulsory component of medical training (and still is in some natural medicine degrees), albeit only one aspect of diagnosis and treatment.

Medical or health astrology concerns particular ways of determining and interpreting an individual's horoscope with particular reference to health issues - diagnosis of current dis-eases, identification of areas of bodily weaknesses, and the prescription of natural cures and remedies. In ancient times, and still even today, the movement of the stars and planets was believed to affect bodily functions, and to cause ailments, or cure them.

During the Middle Ages, many drawings of the 'zodiac man' were made, which showed which signs of the zodiac were related to each part of the body, providing information as to the best times of the year to undertake cures for ailments affecting the corresponding body parts.

Health astrology persists today in many forms and among astrologers themselves, from whom clients seek counsel on health-related issues, and while it certainly cannot be used diagnose a condition or dis-ease, one's Sun sign, along with other factors of the natal chart, can definitely indicate potential problem areas of weakness or possible troubles. This branch of astrology has been found to be surprisingly accurate in most cases. While mostly accurate, none of the following information should ever be used as a substitute for professional medical advice should you be personally concerned about any of the conditions or afflictions listed for your Sun sign.

GEMINIAN HEALTH

Gemini is associated with the Hands, Shoulders, Arms, Hands, Fingers, Clavicle, Sternum, Windpipe and Bronchial Tubes, Lungs, Trachea, Capillaries, Breath, Thoracic Vertebrae, Body Tubing, Nervous System, Upper Ribs, and the Parietal Lobe, Thymus Gland and Pons areas of the Brain, and its natives may suffer from disorders, conditions or accidents to these parts. But the most common ailments are those affecting the nervous system and mental faculties. With a Gemini Sun, you are liable to nervous debility and exhaustion, insomnia, neuritis, mental strain and intense irritability; the chief remedy for these afflictions is to avoid stress, worry and overactivity. Fractures of the arms, hands and collarbones are common, as well as the allergic triad - asthma, eczema and most other allergies. Dairy products should be minimised due to their mucus-forming properties.

Gemini represents the energy of connection and communication. Your nature is hot, moist, quick and nervous. Any form of suppression, physical or mental, is likely to make you ill. Nowhere in the zodiac are body and mind so entwined as in people born under Gemini. The Water Signs Cancer, Scorpio and Pisces, are influenced by their emotions, and these in turn affect their bodies. But you are an intellectual sign, and your mental processes are far swifter than your emotions. Geminis need to rest their busy brains with much more sleep than other mere mortals, but since you are naturally vulnerable to insomnia, you rarely get enough slumber. You of all people must learn to relax totally in mind or body, even if it's only for a few minutes at a time. Negative thoughts or feelings, real or imagined, and confinement or restriction, will also adversely affect your health. Oddly, Gemini will likely suffer emotional breakdowns more easily from boredom and confinement than from overactivity. You need the freedom to move, speak and do as you please. Your living space should be as airy and light as possible. Geminis don't like to be down for long and cannot tolerate being confined to bed or anywhere else, and if bed-bound you are usually restless to the point of exhausting and effectively resigning yourself to the situation. You usually recover quickly, however, and take flight as soon as you can - and often well before.

Because your sign governs the lungs and respiratory system, issues concerning oxygenation of the blood, coughs, colds, influenza, bronchitis, speech problems and other chest or lung complaints are the other most likely causes of ill-health.

Afflictions, injuries and conditions affecting the arms, shoulders, hands and body tubing are also a possibility, as these are all vulnerable areas.

Although not necessarily strong, Geminis are almost certainly wiry and are known as being perpetually young, so generally don't suffer too much with their health. Any difficulties that arise are usually psychologically-based and can be attributed to the vast amounts of nervous energy which may not be burned off properly. Geminis must also guard the health of their lungs as this is one of the susceptible areas, and although smoking is dangerous to everybody, you are particularly prone to the side effects of smoking. This, combined with your lack of thought nor care for tomorrow (it never comes, right?), means that a lung dis-ease which may accumulate over many years, is ignored or unknown until it is too late. Geminis should therefore be particularly careful not to smoke or be exposed to cigarette smoke, even though it may indeed be a fidgety and sociable habit that proves extremely difficult to give up.

It is also essential for you to maintain an optimistic and objective outlook, though this is rarely an effort for you. You should not allow your vivid imagination to take control, as it can quickly raise you to intense peaks of excitement and anticipation, often culminating in nerve-fraying disillusionment and despondency. An unchecked imagination can also induce depression through brooding and worry, and may manifest as unpredictable mood fluctuations.

Your ruling planet Mercury governs the Nervous System, Sensory Nerves, Nerve Fluid, Right Cerebral Hemisphere, Tongue, Bile, Buttocks, Hearing, Speech, Hands and Body Tubing. Mercury is believed to control the whole nervous system, and there is an emphasis on the mental processes, which are usually bright and quick in those under its influence, but also makes you vulnerable to nervousness and unspent restless energy. Mercury is also associated with respiration and the mental faculties, such as memory, and nervous or mental disorders may manifest if you do not take care to nurture your mind's health. Mercury rules the brain and mind; it is changeable in nature. These are all your possible weak spots. As a Mercurial child, you may be afflicted with headaches, speech impediments, all manner of respiratory ailments, poor dietary assimilation, intestinal gas, lung and breathing disorders, asthma, and tinnitus or hearing loss.

Keeping yourself in excellent health overall, with a special awareness of Gemini's vulnerable points, is key to achieving all you set out to do, and getting the most out of your life!

THE CELL SALTS ★ ASTROLOGICAL TONICS

Homeopathy and astrology have colluded to provide a wonderful list of astrological tonics, one particularly suited to each of the twelve signs. These are called 'homeopathic cell salts', 'tissue salts' or 'biochemic cell salts', and are available in most health food stores, are inexpensive and easy to take. They are considered to be gentle, effective and safe, even for children, people in fragile health states, and the elderly. Although the full picture, drawn from a full natal horoscope, gives a fuller, more accurate idea of an individual's unique constitution, even simply working with one's date of birth can be enough for the medical astrologer to suggest the use of a cell salt based upon the correlation with an individual's Sun sign.

As well as the cell salts having a significant effect upon physical ailments, they can also profoundly influence the subtle energy bodies, including the mental, emotional, etheric and spiritual. Although the most common use of these salts is based upon each salt's correspondence with a Sun sign, use of the cell salt related to one's Moon sign can assist with addressing deeper underlying emotional issues, such as anxiety, depression, panic and fear. Use of the cell salt relating to your Moon sign will therefore help to restore your sense of safety, balance, security and emotional resilience. In the first seven years of life, when the Moon is the most influential sphere in our lives, Lunar cell salts are the most appropriate choice as a remedy or tonic.

For specific health problems, take both the salt of your Sun or Moon sign, *and* the salt that pertains to the specific condition. The same principle applies to the Ascendant sign, as the First House represents one's physical health, and especially if the Sun or Moon is a rising planet, which means rulership of the whole chart. For the purposes of this book, however, the cell salt that correlates with your Sun sign only is outlined.

TISSUE SALT FOR GEMINI ★ KALI MUR.

Kalium Muriaticum, or Kali Mur. (Potassium chloride) is the cell salt for Gemini. It is an essential component of muscles, blood, mucous membranes, nerve cells, and brain cells. It serves to regulate the fibrin of the blood and help rapid-thinking Geminis to maintain clarity and focus without burning out. Deficiencies of this tissue salt is often the result of the excretion of minerals through increased urine flow, and any depletion of Kali Mur. will manifest in such conditions as glandular swelling, sinusitis, coating of the tongue, excess mucous discharge and skin scaling. Kali Mur. can be used to clear the residual effects of colds and flu such as fluid in the ear or excessive mucus in the nose or throat. It will help to break down mucous and allow the body to create new tissue through dietary intake, as chronic inflammation of the mucous membranes can occur when the body is unable to break down nutrients, 'excreting' them in the form of mucous run-off. It is essential to the formation of most cells of the body, except the bone cells, and helps cells retain their shape. In the blood, this mineral helps to form fibrin. When there is not enough fibrin in the blood, a thick, white discharge can result. Environmental toxicity can also be alleviated with the use of this tissue salt.

AIR SIGN GEMINI & THE SANGUINE HUMOR

Greek physician Hippocrates (460 - 370 BC) theorised that certain human behaviours were caused by body fluids, called 'humors'. Later, Galen of Pergamon (AD 131 - 200), a Greek physician, developed the first typology of temperaments to encompass many facets of the human psyche and physiology. These also related to the classical elements of Fire, Earth, Air and Water - as choleric, melancholic, sanguine and phlegmatic respectively. According to the Greeks who developed the temperament theory (the word stems from the Latin word *temperamentum*, meaning mixture), temperament is the 'mixture' of qualities that combine to form elements in physics and humors in medicine. The Greeks sought equilibrium in the four qualities of hot, cold, wet (moist), and dry, the elements of Earth, Air, Fire and Water, and the four humors of choler or yellow bile, melancholer or black bile, blood and phlegm. If balance was achieved, the person was said to be well- or even-tempered, and the importance of determining the temperament allowed for imbalances to be treated.

In ancient times, each of the four types of humors corresponded to a different personality type, which were associated with a domination of various biological functions. It was suggested that the temperaments came to clearest manifestation in childhood, between around the ages of six and fourteen of age, after which they become subordinate, but still influential, factors in our personality. It is important to note that your temperament is not your personality. However, your personality can incorporate parts of the temperament in its expression. Personality is shaped by both external and internal factors, whereas the temperament is innate, an inborn, inherent part of each individual.

The Air element corresponds with the humor sanguine, which is characterised by quick, impulsive and relatively short-lived reactions. Sanguine types are analogous with Air, which is the main element in spring, the season with which this temperament has an affinity. Sanguine characters are ruled by Venus and Jupiter, hence the labels Venusian and Jupiterian Sanguines.

Sanguine types are driven by the need for attention and acceptance, social contact, relating, relationships, and trying to impress others. A sanguine disposition represents positivity, optimism, extroversion, expressiveness, talkativeness, and light-heartedness. You are generally responsive, carefree, easygoing and lively.

Overall, a sanguine disposition represents sociability and openness. Its taste is bitter, its nature acidic, its indication blood. The sanguine humor is associated with the *gas* ^ body, and with hot and moist conditions.

---

^ A couple of thousand years ago, the Mesopotamians, Chinese and Egyptians, and more recently the Arabs, practised a medicine called 'of three bodies'. According to the doctors of the ancient world (who often practised as astrologers as well), a human being had three bodies: the physical body, the ethereal (or vital) body and the astral body, imparting a holistic approach to health. In modern medicine, usually only the physical body is focused upon fully. According to tradition, this physical body comprises three principles or states corresponding to three primordial elements: *solid* (Earth), *liquid* (Water) and *gas* (Air). This is the material body, the physical outer cover of muscles, nerves and organs held together by the skeleton. The Fire element corresponds with the *astral* body, which sits outside the physical body in one's auric field.

MONEY ATTRIBUTES

Colour for Increased Earning Power ★ Yellow

The following plants can be used by all zodiac signs to assist in attracting money ★ Ginger, Allspice, Clover, Orange, Marjoram, Cinnamon, Sassafras, Woodruff, Bergamot, Tonka Beans, Heliotrope, Alfalfa, Coltsfoot, Thyme, Mace, Irish Moss, Clove, Almond, Corn, Honeysuckle, Sesame, Nutmeg, Vetiver, Poppy, Jasmine, Dill and Elder Flower. To attract luck and success, try using any of the above, combined with any of the following: Alfalfa Seeds, Basil, Mustard Seeds, Vervain Leaves, Poppy Seeds, Rosemary, Lemon, Anise and Holly.

Striving for financial gain and abundance with a healthy inner moral compass is, in my view, one of the most noble goals we can set for ourselves. When we have more money, we are better placed to help ourselves and of course others; after all, as Abraham Maslow's Hierarchy of Needs model (1943) attests, once our primary and base survival needs have been satisfied, we can then advance higher towards loftier achievements, such as self-confidence, creativity and self-actualisation. Prosperity allows us to turn our attention to these more transcendental matters - to reach for lives not just of material comfort and luxuries, but of meaning, generosity, balance, harmony, fulfilment and joy. Our Sun sign can offer clues as to how we go about acquiring, earning, saving, maintaining, and allowing the overall flow of giving and receiving money. What's *your* money style?

Your finances will flow best where turnover is quick or for work done on commission or piece-work, rather than a settled salary. Your clever ideas can often make you money too. Although you are adaptable to any financial situation, you must guard against being fickle and becoming bored with ventures that require time, patience and endurance, to ensure money does not slip through your fingers.

Being gregarious and generous, you share your money with others but can be somewhat careless in holding onto it for long periods of time. With little foresight or thought for tomorrow, you often live for the moment and spend whatever is in your pocket at the time. Banks can be a foreign concept to you, as not only do they waste your precious time and energy by making you stand in queues, saving money for a rainy day or unexpected misfortune is alien to you. Bright, clever and imaginative as you are, you are impractical with money. You have a happy-go-lucky streak which sees money fall into your lap through sheer chance, but make sure that you don't acquire a reputation for forgetting to pay debts. It's not that you mean to forget, it's usually just that you tend to have so many other things on your mind.

Calculations, budgets and spreadsheets are not your idea of fun, particularly if you have to concentrate or sit still for a period of time, but they are imperative for the scatterbrained Gemini, who will forget what he has walked into the supermarket for in the first place, and end up with a basket-full of unnecessary things which were not on his list (if he made one in the first place).

To counter boredom and receive through a variety of sources, many Geminis may spread their money over a number of different types of investments and hobbies. Money in the bank is not important to Gemini, who is resourceful and always able to raise cash when required, even if by questionable means (remember that Gemini is the smooth-talking trickster conman of the zodiac); in fact, Gemini invented the get-rich-scheme concept and the financial con. Although quick-witted and acutely intelligent, it would do you well to remember the saying "a fool and his money are soon parted", because it particularly applies to the Gemini and relationship with his wallet.

You show no hesitation in borrowing money and lending in return, and never worry about running up enormous debts on a credit card. A natural gambler and shrewd, clever investor, Gemini will have a flutter - and usually wins on the gamble.

COLOURS

Chromatomancy, or divination by colour, is a form of energy therapy that has been used for thousands of years by many different cultures. It works on the principle that we make both instinctive and rational choices or preferences based on circumstances which are already present in ourselves; colour also has an effect on the energy in an environment, and we in turn respond consciously or subconsciously to our surroundings. If we look at the causes, and try to understand the reasons, as to why we are so receptive to one particular colour over another, we will see that there is a subtle link between certain hues and our emotional and instinctive individual reactions. The colour which we give to things results from a combination of three elements:

1. The light or the vibration of a body;

2. The context in which it is found and the interaction between its own light and that of its environment;

3. The sensitivity of the eye's retina which sees the body in question. Because of this, a colour can vary, depending on the individual's perceptions, namely, his sensitivity, his mood, and his view of reality. For a long time, people have understood that their vision of reality depends a lot on their moods, feelings and emotions.

Chromatotherapy, or colour healing, stems from this body of evidence, and its main application is the use of colours for healing purposes. Colours are generally associated with characteristics, feelings, stones, metals, plants and flowers, planets and even the zodiac signs. In varying cultures, they play a significant role in ceremonies and regalia.

We vibrate to the frequency of colour, shown through its continual movement and change in our aura ^. One of the most beautiful examples of colour is the rainbow. This architect of colour is caused by the refraction and internal reflection of light in raindrops. Colour can be perceived as either a pigment, or as illumination. The colour spectrum can be divided into eight main colours: red, orange, yellow, green, turquoise, blue, violet and magenta. Each colour has a wavelength and frequency that carry different therapeutic qualities which have indirect effects upon our health and bodily systems, and because of this, coupled with the fact that we as living energy centres emanate colour, colour can be a great medium in healing, calming, energising, increasing and attracting.

Aristotle, in the fourth century BCE, considered blue and yellow to be the true primary colours and related them to life's polarities: Sun and Moon, male and female, stimulation and sedation, in and out, expansion and contraction. He also associated colours with the four elements of Fire, Earth, Air and Water. Hippocrates, the father of medicine, used colour extensively in medicinal healing and recognised that the therapeutic effects of a white violet differed from those of a purple one. In the fifteenth century, Paracelsus placed particular importance on the role of colour in healing.

Each Sun sign and planetary body has a specific colour or colours which when used in combination with wishing rituals, can enhance their power immensely. Coloured candles can be used to good effect, as the fire energy of the flame/s increases the power of any wish, and flames are also a useful aid to meditating on, focusing upon or clarifying what you want. Coloured candles help to focus the energy for whatever purpose the colour is in sympathy with (e.g. green for money, pink for romance, orange for joy, etc.)

With all this in mind, wearing or using your Sun sign or ruling planet's magical colour/s on a regular basis will undoubtedly bring great benefits.

^ The aura is defined as an energy field, which interpenetrates with, and radiates beyond, the physical body. Clairvoyantly seen, the aura is full of light, colour and shade. The trained healer or seer sees or senses indications within the aura as to the spiritual, physical and emotional state of the individual. Much of the auric colour and energy emanates from the chakras.

YOUR LUCKY COLOURS

For Gemini ★ Silver, White, Dove-Grey, Light Green, Yellow, Pale Yellow (balance with a Light Mauve), White with Red Spots

For Mercury ★ Yellow, Jade Green

The sign of the Twins likes to circulate and communicate. Your colour is the yellow of summer sunshine, energy and Mercury, which bursts forth like your character in a social setting.

Each of the eight colours of the rainbow spectrum also has a complementary colour to which it is matched. Red is complementary to turquoise, orange to blue, yellow to violet, and green to magenta. If these colour pairs enhance each other's most spellbinding qualities and energies, perhaps you could try wearing your Sun sign's lucky colour with its matching complementary colour in order to produce extra magical results! Your lucky Geminian colours are silver and yellow, which complements violet. Now you know your colours, you can dress for success!

FEATURE COLOURS ★ SILVER & YELLOW

★ SILVER ★

Planetary Association ★ The Moon

Healing Qualities ★ Happiness, Prosperity, Prestige, Opulence, Wisdom, Purging Negativity, Luck, Femininity

Keywords ★ Channelling, Clairvoyance, Astral Energies, Moon, Silver Birch, Amulets, Wisdom

The colour of the Moon, silver can be used for astral or dream work, practising scrying (crystal ball gazing or divination) and for wish magic. Because of its associations with the Moon, silver is also connected with femininity and feminine power. Silver has been revered as a mystical metal since the dawn of civilisation. Ancient alchemists regarded it to be especially valuable and attempted to transmute other metals to produce it *. They used the symbol of the Moon to represent this metal (identified in the Periodic Table of Elements as 'Ag'), which they named 'luna'. Silver, being linked with the Third Eye chakra, is useful for channelling energy, both of a psychic nature and, in more practical terms, of electricity and heat. Silver has also come to represent quality, class and style, as the expressions 'silver service' and 'born with a silver spoon in mouth' exemplify. It also embodies the wisdom gained by learning through experience and optimism, through questing for a 'silver lining' in the face of life's adversities. Mirrors are flat silver-coloured surfaces that reflect all light.

Since medieval times, mirrors have been used by clairvoyants and other diviners to make contact with mystical spirits and foretell the future, back then leading to the belief that parallel worlds were hidden behind mirrors, something which Lewis Carroll's literary Alice explores in her *Through the Looking Glass* adventures. When people and some animals grow older, their hair loses its original colour and turns silver. Someone who is older is more likely to have more knowledge, which is why the colour silver also relates to wisdom. Chinese feng shui is based on the principles of the five elements. Silver is a strong metallic element and as such has powerful Chi qualities. According to theory, it can be used to support the Water element, but destroys Wood. Another potent silver association is that in heraldry, metallic silver paint is called argent. The word 'argent' inspired the country name Argentina, because the first European explorers reported seeing a huge silver mountain there. Silver overall corresponds with that which is of material value, versatility, liveliness and higher levels of consciousness.

* Alchemists believed that mercury was the substance used in creation. They thought that this element was a particular type of silver which is why they called mercury 'quicksilver'.

★ YELLOW ★

Planetary Association ★ Mercury

Complementary Colour ★ Violet

Healing Qualities ★ Self-confidence, Optimism, Happiness, Life Force, Brightness, Energy, Cheerfulness, Long-term Memory, Nervous System

Keywords ★ Sunniness, the Sun, Vitality, Energy, Healing, Intellect, Confidence, Eloquence, Travel, Movement, Enthusiasm, Creative Imagination, Communication, Upbeat, Open-mindedness, Philosophy, Attraction, Charm, Persuasion

Yellow is a colour of the Sun and can also represent Air or Earth. It is a bright and happy colour, uplifting and energising your emotions and inspiring the mind and spirit. Yellow brings hope and cheer and is a high-visibility colour that can signal danger, being used in hazard signs, albeit to a lesser extent than red. It is used for mental stimulation, improving the memory, communication, travel and even wealth. Yellow is an optimistic, warm, dynamic colour that encourages positivity and inner power. It strengthens the nervous system and soothes stress-related tension. Yellow is the dominant colour of the Solar Plexus centre in our body's chakra system and is related to the mind and intellect, power and control. When in balance, it endows you with a positive outlook - free, self-confident and happy. Bridging the gap between the emotions and the intellect, it promotes dynamism and increased creativity. Yellow represents the nervous system which it is said to stimulate, tonify and strengthen.

A yellow environment is a powerful space in which to work or grow, so is an ideal choice when one wishes to increase positive vibes, versatility, energy, self-expression and creativity. Yellow, representing the power of thought and stimulating mental activity, makes it a good colour to have in a study or work environment. It dispels fear and melancholy, being emotionally healing and lively. Being the colour of detachment, it can also help us to detach from unhelpful thoughts, feelings and habits. Yellow has many 'happy' associations, such as daffodils, sunflowers, the robes of Buddhists and Hindus *, and prosperity, in both a material and spiritual sense. In both colour and crystal therapies, yellow, with its summery disposition and associations, can help alleviate the symptoms of seasonal affective disorder (SAD). Overall, yellow rays carry positive magnetic currents which are inspiring and stimulating, and these currents strengthen the nerves, impart vitality and stimulate the higher mind.

* Yellow is associated with enlightenment, which is why Buddhists and Hindus wear yellow robes.

Yellow and violet, its complementary rainbow spectrum complementary colour, as well as silver, are Gemini's special LUCKY colours! The three can be worn or otherwise used together to dazzling and mesmerising effect.

GEMINI'S CHAKRA CORRESPONDENCE ★ THROAT

The word 'chakra' comes from the Sanskrit and means 'wheel', disc' or 'circle'. Chakras are vitally important to your physical health, emotional wellbeing and spiritual growth, and are regarded as a complete integrated system that works holistically. The chakras are funnel-shaped spinning energy vortexes of multi-coloured light. These swirling vortexes of energy absorb and distribute life-force, the subtle energy known as *prana*. The seven master chakras - Root, Sacral, Solar Plexus, Heart, Throat, Third Eye and Crown - lie in the centre line of the body, with the first five embedded within the spinal column. Each chakra vibrates at a different vibrational frequency and on a different note, and responds to specific life issues or 'thought forms'.

The lower body chakras deal with physical issues. As we move up the body, the chakras correspond to increasingly spiritual concerns. As a consequence, each chakra's energy vibrates at a different rate, depending on whether they govern earthbound or ethereal issues. The lower chakras have slower and denser vibrations, while the higher chakras spin at faster speeds with higher vibrations.

Because the chakras have no physical manifestation and cannot be located using any scientific instrument, they have tended to be viewed with scepticism by many Western medical professionals, a distinction they share with energy points in acupuncture and the notion of meridians. Instead, they are believed to have been sensed intuitively by many people over many centuries, and indeed people in yoga positions and in deep meditation have reported experiencing the sensation of a surge of energy rising from the base of the spine and emerging through the top of the head. Some people have even said they have seen points of blue light when their *kundalini* energy has risen from the lowest chakra to the highest, as well as experiencing a profound sense of happiness and ecstasy.

In summary, the Universal Life Force enters the body through the Crown chakra at the top of the head. As it works its way through the body, it flows through the other centres. As it spreads to the Base chakra, it is said to arouse the kundalini energy, which yogis believe sleeps in a coiled serpentine form.

The chakra associated with Gemini is the fifth, or Throat chakra, which governs self-expression, speech and communication, and corresponds to our beliefs, thoughts and actions involving communicating with others.

THROAT CHAKRA

Location ★ Throat Region
Colour ★ Blue
Concerned with ★ Communication, Speech & Self-Expression
Gland ★ Thyroid
Essential Oils ★ Cajeput, Blue Chamomile, Elemi, Cypress, Myrrh, Eucalyptus, Palmarosa, Ravensara, Black Pepper, Rosemary, Yarrow, Sage
Animals ★ Bull, Elephant, Lion
Shape ★ Downward Triangle
Element ★ Spirit/Ether
Planet ★ Mercury
Zodiac Signs ★ Gemini, Virgo
Flower ★ 16-petalled Lotus
Energy State ★ Vibration
Mantra ★ HAM

Positive Expression ★ Spiritual, self-expressive, willing to work with the Divine, articulate, cooperative, effective communication

Negative Expression (Blockage) ★ Indecisive or wilful, idealistic versus realistic, arrogant, deceptive to self or others, judgemental, problems with self-expression (expression of own truths), inability to communicate ideas or uncontrolled, low-value or inconsistent communication, problems with creativity, manipulative

The Throat chakra is located at the base of the throat. Its Sanskrit name is *vishuddha*, and its symbol is a sixteen-petal blue lotus flower whose centre contains a downward-pointing triangle within which is a circle representing the full Moon. Balance in this chakra is expressed as easy communication with ourselves and others on all levels. It corresponds to the thyroid and parathyroid glands and the pharyngeal nerve plexus. Crystals that can be used to cleanse and balance this chakra are mostly blue stones, including: Blue Lace Agate, Amazonite, Blue Fluorite, Chrysocolla, Blue Chalcedony, Angelite, Aquamarine, Azeztulite, Azurite, Blue Calcite, Larimar, Lapiz Lazuli, Aqua Aura Quartz, Malachite, Blue Sapphire, Turquoise and Blue Tourmaline. Amber also helps cleanse and balance this area.

LUCKY CAREER TIPS & PATHS THAT WILL MAKE YOUR BANK BALANCE & SPIRITUAL SELF SOAR

The branch of astrology known as 'vocational astrology' encompasses the areas of one's calling, career path, or ideal profession. Careers, jobs, professions and occupations can all mean different things to different people, but to simplify the definition, I refer to a vocation as one's true calling, one's authentic path, and a dynamic way of life which pays an income in some form and leads to a deep fulfilment of personal and spiritual needs. An ideal vocation will provide self fulfilment, ego satisfaction, and feed one's inner drive to achieve what they ultimately wish to achieve, whether that be to gain recognition, wealth or approval, to travel, to learn and fulfil an inner need for knowledge, an urge to serve others in some way, or an urge to improve personal, societal or Universal conditions.

In order to gain ultimate fulfilment and self-esteem, we all need a purpose in life. Many people gain this through their work, providing the job or career they choose suits their temperament, talents and aspirations. If our professional life is unsatisfactory or disharmonious in any way, frustration, unhappiness and even despair can result. Although your whole horoscope would need to be drawn up and interpreted in order to gain more substantial, deeper insights into your ideal career and purpose, you can begin by being guided by your Sun sign, which can give you many pointers to a suitable, and therefore successful, career path. You just never know, something in the following might jump out at you and make your soul dance immediately - and hopefully all the way to the bank!

"You're sure to find a Gemini or two skimming through the halls and matching wits with people in a radio station, a public relations firm, a publishing house, a telephone answering service, an auto showroom or an advertising agency ... when you've found this quicksilver person, study him carefully ... the first thing you'll notice is a nervous energy that fairly snaps, crackles and pops in the air around him."
Linda Goodman

With your Sun in Gemini, your greatest talents are mental and physical agility, wit, versatility, swiftness, and usually excellent verbal or written communicative skills. Since your ruling planet Mercury is also a trickster, you are capable of bringing a humorous and breezy touch to even the tensest situation. Running on raw nerves a lot of the time, you need to learn how to be alone and capitalise on solitude, as well as sufficient sleep to be at your best. Your ideal vocation gives you variety, mental stimulation, novelty, interaction with other people, and uses your dexterity and wit.

Occupations involving travel and familiarity with a number of different environments would suit the Gemini temperament. Because 'variety is the spice of life' for you, travelling and being in new, ever-changing surroundings can bring excitement and happiness to your professional self. You are the most likely of all the zodiac signs to have more than a few careers during your lifetime - sometimes even three at once! Indeed, being a Gemini gives you an unmatched versatility and sense of curiosity which means that at any one time you may have several fingers in several pies. With this, there is an ever-present danger that you will flit from one job to another without ever mastering or specialising in anything.

Gemini endows you with a sharp mind which can function in almost any type of field, but you must first consider some essential points in your choice of work. Firstly, it must be mentally stimulating and offer some degree of variety and flexibility; and secondly, it should connect you with other people and ideas on a constant basis. This is important for two reasons: Gemini, being the hallmark of communication, needs to be in consistent contact with others, either physically, mentally, verbally or through travel, books, magazines, email, the internet, or almost any other form of correspondence and exchange.

There are many fields which involve various types of communication and correspondence and which would suit the Geminian spirit, such as: Driver, Courier, Writer, Lecturer, Politician, Public Speaker, Sales Representative, Teacher, Tutor, Travel Consultant, Professor, Coach or Trainer.

Geminis, possessing good manual dexterity and use of your hands, also make excellent Designers, Manicurists, Craftspeople, Engravers, Tattooists, Commercial Artists, Composers, Surgeons, Osteopaths, Sculptors, and Instrumentalists. These are just a few of the multitude of occupations which allow you to express yourself through the use of your hands and quick, agile mind. Any profession that disseminates knowledge or that capitalises on your ability to use your hands to 'create' or fix, is therefore perfect for you.

For Geminis, the following fields may also hold appeal: Journalism, Communication, Travel, Transport, Agencies, Teaching, Publishing, Advertising, Printing, Secretarial or Clerical Work, Broadcasting, Commentary, Linguistics, Chauffeur, Telephone Operator, Translator, Interpreter, Postman and Navigator.

Perhaps the career best suited to Gemini is that of a salesperson. With your verbal skills, you can run rings around others, and your ability to exaggerate effortlessly enables you to convince even the most sophisticated, discerning or cynical buyer to purchase your product or accept your offer. Even better, a travelling salesperson position would suit your love of travel, movement, 'mind food', mobility and need for new surroundings.

Furthermore, your love of words often leads you into the field of journalism, and the seriously intellectual Gemini is capable of becoming an eminent scientific researcher, high-ranking professor or inspirational teacher. Having the gift of the gab and ample character and charm, you can also be a successful politician or actor, though your energy and interest seldom last beyond the 'campaign' or the promotion of the play. Indeed in politics, you would go to any length to defeat an opponent, using gossip, scandals and lies if necessary, and your Mutable nature allows you to support whatever platform seems appropriate to the audience you are addressing at the time.

Although you are happy to take on positions of power and authority, these qualities don't come all that naturally to you, and you find it lonely at the top; it is a rare Gemini who prefers to work alone, or indeed to court power or profound influence. Social status, definitely, but highbrow authority, no.

Overall, the career options for Geminis are literally endless and limitless, as your intellect and manual prowess are boundless, and endow you with the very unique capacity to quite literally be a 'jack of all trades'. There is very little the Twins cannot set their mind to and master. The professional world is your oyster!

LUCKY PLACES WHERE YOUR ENERGY IS HEIGHTENED

As the Air element and sanguine humor corresponds with hot and moist conditions, warm, humid, tropical places suit your constitution, disposition and temperament. The following nations, countries and cities are also places whose vibrations are closely allied with the sign of Gemini: Canada, Morocco, the Maldives, Lower Egypt, St Lucia, Belgium, Wales, Armenia, Sardinia, United States (New York and San Francisco), Sweden, England (London), Greece, Italy (Lombardy), Spain (Cordoba), Tunisia, Ecuador, Bermuda, South Africa, Tonga, Germany (Nuremberg), Angola, Eritrea, Guyana, Iceland, Gibraltar, Kuwait, St Pierre and Miquelon, Norway, and Switzerland. City centres and educational establishments are also in tune with the Geminian energy, as are libraries and disco halls. A fun-filled tour with friends and strangers alike, visiting all the party capitals of the world such as Ibiza, Los Angeles or the Greek Islands, and all places which fulfil your insatiable curiosity, fun-loving nature, need for knowledge, and childlike sense of wonder, such as Disneyland, Bollywood or Magic Kingdom, and could very well be your ticket to Geminian heaven!

GEMS & CRYSTALS

"People love stones, and apparently stones love people. Like the angels they may be, they seem endlessly willing to serve the wellbeing of humans and to help us achieve our desires …Unlike people of the ancient past, we now have access to virtually the entire mineral kingdom. We have the opportunity to work like modern alchemists, combining and arranging the stones and their currents, looking for combinations and patterns that can help us enhance our inner and outer lives."

Robert Simmons, *Stones of the New Consciousness*

Each crystal and mineral of the Earth embodies different qualities, patterns or potential expressions of the Divine language, the silent whispers of the Universe. If we can accept the fact that the human body is a sophisticated, multi-faceted antenna system comprised of a crystalline matrix that is constantly transmitting and receiving all manner of energies, it could then be assumed that energy and body workers who use quartz, shells and stones, which are also crystalline materials, have the power to promote resonant interactions with the liquid 'crystal' structures found in human tissues. It could even be said that we are all made of essentially the same substances and structures, and that crystals and gemstones vibrate at varying energetic levels which can connect with our own in order to 'buzz' and dance together to make a harmonious Universe both within and without.

All crystals work through vibrational balancing and by channelling energy. The magic of crystals is in their colour, which is determined by the rate at which their atoms vibrate; these vibrations can be matched to the energy given by your own body's aura. And just as light can be focused and refracted through gemstones, so too can all kinds of psychic energy, from healing energies to Divine communications.

Gemstones can help us attune to higher vibrations and bring them into our own experience and being. This theory of crystal resonance suggests that the characteristic energy patterns emanated by any stone can be transferred into the 'liquid crystal medium' of our bodies through resonance. Our bodies, being composed of these tuneable liquids, can mimic and mirror any consistent vibrational pattern with which we come into contact; we can therefore resonate with the healthful qualities of various crystals and minerals.

Crystals and precious stones have been valued throughout world cultures over many centuries for their healing virtues and capacities to imbue courage, strength, invulnerability, clairvoyance, love and numerous other qualities. Wearing gemstones is one of the simplest and most effective self-healing practices you can undertake, and wearing or carrying those stones whose vibrations correspond with the qualities you wish to embody brings their energetic currents into engagement with your body.

Over time the phenomenon of energetic integration, may be felt tangibly and your own vibrational field may internalise the stone's currents and adjust to them and effectively 'store' them, making them, eventually, a part of your own vibrational make-up. And we seem to know from the resonances we feel within our bodies when in contact with these gemstones, that crystals emanate tangible, if oft immeasurable, currents.

Crystals act as transmitters and amplifiers of your will or intentions - as long as your will or intentions are in sympathy with the crystal's energy. The mineral kingdom refers to stones, minerals and crystals and the associations and vibrations they carry. When working with stones, we are working with several different layers of spiritual energies, and although they can be regarded as inanimate 'psychic batteries', they are actually moving, vibrating masses of energy which transmit potential and power into our lives. Some crystals and stones even have receptive powers, which means they can absorb energy and retain it within until cleansed or re-programmed.

Although it is untrue that the only stones you can usefully wear are the ones astrologically matched with your Sun sign or ruling planet, those which align with your Sun sign or ruling planet are your most fortuitous and therefore strongest 'attractors' and 'amplifiers'.

Twelve oracular gemstones were described in the Bible, as the author of *Exodus* (28-15 and 17-21) knew them. Yahweh spoke to Moses about the breastplate he would have to wear to train for priesthood, and described it to him in these words: "And thou shalt make the breastplate of judgement with cunning work; ... And thou shalt set in it settings of stones, even four rows of stones; the first row shall be a sardius, a topaz, and a carbuncle. And the second row shall be an emerald, a sapphire and a diamond. And the third row an opal, an agate and an amethyst. And the fourth row a beryl, and an onyx, and a jasper; they shall be set in hold in their inclosings. And the stones shall be with the children ... (all) twelve (of them)." Given that the compilers of the Bible lived during a time when astrological belief was prevalent in Babylon, it seems valid to assert that these previously named gemstones would have some astrological basis. Further, since these ancient people supposedly made correlations between each of the twelve precious stones, and one of the twelve zodiac signs, there are seven crystalline systems set down in crystallography (or the science of the laws which influence the formation, structure and geometric, physical and chemical properties of crystallised matter) as analogous with the seven traditional ruling planets of the zodiac.

However, nobody is under the rule of one planet alone. We are all in essence a complex mixture of every planet, many elements and varying aspects, depending on their positions, placements and prominence in our birth chart. Everything that goes on in the skies above us affects what is going on here on Earth, and also *within* us. Your lucky stones are to assist you to tune into your Sun sign's energy and planetary influences, but you are by no means limited to the ones listed for your sign alone. Above all, let your stones, whichever ones you choose, work for you and allow them to transport your very own unique and magical energy into the wider Universe.

> "Beautiful and strong is the material of stones, but more beautiful and much more powerful is the mystery that emanates from them."
>
> **Chinese Poet & Alchemist, Li Po, 8th Century A.D.**

★ CLEAR QUARTZ ★

The Master Healer ★ *For All Zodiac Signs*

A common, well-known and popular gem, clear quartz (sometimes known as rock crystal) is an all-purpose 'jack-of-all-trades' stone. It amplifies the magic of any work you do or wishes you make. It is connected with all the chakras and increases the power of all other crystals. Clear quartz is a deep soul cleanser, which unblocks and regulates energy and emotions on all levels. It is balancing and harmonising. In various cultures, quartz crystal is reputed to be the most powerful crystal, the 'grandfather crystal', and the 'chief of the Stone People'. Clear quartz is also considered to be the only gemstone that is modifiable to suit your needs *, as other crystals automatically contain and retain their own specific resonance or natural signature. In essence, clear quartz is the most easily programmable and the most overall healing and readily accessible crystals of the mineral kingdom, holding a unique importance in the Universe of gems. And because of its all-encompassing nature and wide-ranging healing abilities, it has zodiacal affinities with all the signs.

* To program your clear quartz crystal, simply hold it on your Third Eye chakra (between and just above the physical eyes) and concentrate on the purpose for which you wish to use it. Be positive and receptive while you

allow your crystal to fill with this energy. If you wish, you could also state the intention of the programming out loud, for example, 'I program this crystal for love / healing / meditation / abundance / protection or (insert your own word here)'. You could also run your clear quartz crystal under running water, allow it to dry naturally, then hold the stone with both hands, bring it up to your mouth and blow into it sharply three times in order to impregnate it with your own breath. Then, hold it firmly in one hand and silently invite and welcome it into your life as a friend, helper and guide.

GEMINIAN & MERCURIAL LUCKY CRYSTALS, STONES & GEMS

Gemini birth stones ★ Alexandrite, Agate, Citrine

May birth stones ★ Agate, Emerald, Tourmaline, Chrysoprase

June birth stones ★ Emerald, Pearl, Moonstone

Alexandrite, Agate, Citrine (your three primary birthstones), Emerald (Mercury), Tourmaline, Chrysoprase, Pearl and Moonstone (May and June birthstones) are your luckiest stones, and at least one of these gems should be worn about your person to ensure good luck and increase your overall magnetism. Serpentine, Hematite, Aquamarine, Calcite, Tiger's Eye, Chrysocolla, Apophyllite, Noble or Iridescent Opal, Rainbow Quartz, Hyaline Quartz, Colourless Tourmaline, Apatite, Celestine, Celestite, Marble, Tibetan Quartz, Titanium Quartz, Blue Spinel, Goldstone, Green Obsidian, Zoisite, Variscite, Topaz, Ulexite, Epidote, Dendritic Agate, Sapphire, Tourmilated and Rutilated Quartz, Jade, Diamond, and all gems that sparkle brilliantly are also in harmony with Geminian energy.

CRYSTALS & THE PLANETS

All the Vedic texts agree in relating gems to planets. This verse from the *Jatax Parijat* links each gem to a planet:

'The ruby is the gem of the Lord of the Day (the Sun),
The shining pearl is the gem of the cold Moon,
Red coral is the gem of Mars,
The emerald is the gem of noble Mercury,
Yellow sapphire is the gem of Jupiter, instructor of gods,
Diamond is the gem of Venus, instructor of demons,
Blue sapphire is the gem of Saturn.'

Each planet influences its gem, and their curative power varies according to the position of its planet in the zodiac. Ayurvedic medicine has always paid attention to these details in their healing practices, often advising people to wear their corresponding zodiacal stone as a ring or a talisman.

CRYSTALS & THE ELEMENTS

Crystals are inextricably linked to the four elements, from their original creation to their potency and use in magical rituals and healing. Formed by the combination, in varying conditions, of different physical elements, such as metals, non-metals and gases, some stones require the enormous heat generated by volcanoes or deep thermal currents to bond their molecular makeup, while others may require pressure or water sources. The effects of the four elements of Fire, Earth, Air and Water is evident in these formation processes. The heat generated by Fire, pressure from the Earth, and the chemical reactions involved in absorbing elements from the Air and Water, all demonstrate the four elements in action to produce the correct conditions and ingredients necessary for the creation of crystals, lending them each their unique qualities.

CRYSTALS & THE AIR ELEMENT

The influence of the Air element may seem less apparent as its effects often occur invisibly, but its nature and essence are very important to some crystals. The most obvious manifestation of Air is in filling spaces; such as bubbles in crystals or the hollows in geodes. Air also provides the elements necessary for chemical reactions to occur during crystal formation. As the element of the intellect, knowledge, mind and clarity, symbolically Air can also fill you with ideas and enhance mental focus. Airy crystals can therefore assist in the formulation of concepts and plans, to focus your thoughts and to make decisions.

Some Airy crystals are ★ Sapphire, Kunzite, Chalcedony, Turquoise, Lapis Lazuli, Agate, Sodalite, Opal and Rose Quartz.

THE CRYSTALLINE SYSTEM OF YOUR RULING PLANET MERCURY

Associated with your ruling planet Mercury, are Tiger's Eye, Jasper, Agate, Coral, Beryl, Azurite, Sardonyx, Gypsum and Marcasite. This is the seventh crystalline system, which is analogous with Mercury, and is known as the monoclinical or clinorhombic system, that is having an oblique prism on a diamond-shaped base. The stone which perhaps represents this system best is Azurite, or copper hydrocarbonate.

MERCURY'S GEMSTONE ASSOCIATION

★ EMERALD ★

"The Emerald is one of the precious stones with the greatest gift of curative power because it is effective against all human frailties and disabilities; in fact, it is the Sun which creates it and its entire substance is made from the vitality of the air."
Extract from *The Works of St Hildegarde of Bingen*

Emerald is a vivid grass-green precious stone belonging to the beryl family, whose name is derived from the Greek *beryllos*, meaning a green stone. Emerald is mainly blue-green in colour but can also be green-yellow and even yellow. Virtues ascribed to this stone are that of hope, purity, prosperity, love, dreams, kindness, healing, fertility and eternal youth; the ancients believed that it would bestow immortality and good fortune upon those who wore it. With its dazzling green brilliance, emerald has long been prized for its magical properties and as such has a long history of myth and folklore. Most important of all was emerald's reputation as a link with the Divine forces. It is said to enhance psychic abilities and clairvoyance. Emerald is a powerful stone, associated with natural elements such as the Moon, rain and water. It is also linked with alchemists and with Hermes, and its legendary healing powers are said to be closely linked to the occult. The ancients believed that the Greek god Hermes inscribed the laws of 'magic', the thirteen precepts, upon an emerald tablet, and indeed, emeralds were dedicated to Mercury, the winged messenger, by early astrologers.

Connected with the Heart chakra, emerald opens and activates this vital organ to heal all problems associated with the heart, whether they be physical or emotional. It is known as 'the stone of successful love' with which unconditional love can be pledged to a partner. Possessing a very loving vibration, emerald carried in the left pocket is said to attract this vibe to you. To increase the loving vibration of your interaction with others, i.e. what you send out, carry this stone in your right pocket. By promoting harmony and wholeness to every aspect of one's life, emerald dispels negativity and draws beauty, wisdom and healing to it. Emerald ensures emotional, physical and mental equilibrium and imparts strength of character to overcome setbacks and misfortunes. As a stone of regeneration and recovery, it can inspire a deep inner knowing, broaden vision, and enhance one's wisdom and integrity. Indeed, in ancient times, emerald was seen as a stone which could deliver knowledge of mysteries, bringing particular wisdom and inspiration, and served both as a remedy and a miracle stone. It encourages us to follow the laws of nature and, by imbuing us with a sense of beauty and openness, enhances our ability to appreciate the wonders of life.

Emeralds were a prime source of wealth in Ancient Greece and Egypt, and this legacy endures today. Emerald is believed to attract good fortune and encourages gratitude, helping you to recognise abundance in all forms rather than just monetary. Perfect, sellable emerald stones are rare; most are cloudy, unremarkable or otherwise flawed, but can still be effectively used for healing purposes. Life-affirming and inspirational, this brilliant green beryl instils a sense of vitality and energy and is an overall uplifting and healing tonic for the mind, body and spirit.

★ **Cinnabar Quartz** ★ Alchemy, magic, transformation, wealth, insight, manifestation and mental agility are all key words for this mixture of red cinnabar, white quartz and other trace minerals. Its element is Fire and it is connected with the Base, Sacral and Third Eye chakras. A very attractive stone, its colour is usually vermilion or scarlet red. It forms around volcanic vents and hot springs and may also occur in sedimentary rocks associated with recent volcanic activity. Cinnabar becomes cinnabar quartz when it forms in conjunction with quartz, and cinnabar quartz is the most beneficial form of cinnabar for metaphysical use. The quartz serves to increase the durability of the stone, as well as magnifying cinnabar's energetic properties. As a stone of the Magician archetype, cinnabar (or cinnabar quartz) can facilitate the alignment of personal will with Divine will, allowing one to 'tweak' the Divine currents so that one can influence the form of creative material manifestation. Cinnabar is also aligned with the god Mercury, also known as Hermes or Thoth, and as such it can help increase mental agility, intellectual brilliance and clarity of thought, traits for which these gods were known.

The usual colour of cinnabar, pure red, is resonant with the colour of one of the images of the Philosopher's Stone, the 'attainment' of which is the goal of alchemy. This is the Stone of the 'lovers of wisdom' (*philo* = love; *sopher* = wisdom, or Sophia), which helps the alchemists attain one of their loftiest aims aside from transmuting lead to gold - that of wisdom. For one's aspirations of spiritual growth and evolution, Cinnabar is a potent quickener, helping to speed up the process by which one's transformation occurs. Overall, it facilitates the process of alchemical change within the individual and brings about the experience and expression of one's newfound inner golden illuminated awareness.

* Cinnabar and Cinnabar Quartz contain Mercury, so caution should be exercised when handling this crystal.

GEMINI'S FEATURE CRYSTAL ★ ALEXANDRITE

Alexandrite is a variety of chrysoberyl, a beryllium aluminium oxide with a hardness of 8.5.

One of the hardest gemstones, second only to diamond and corundum, its crystal pattern is orthorhombic. Alexandrite is a crystal of contrasts. It opens the intuition and metaphysical abilities, and creates a strong will and personal magnetism. One of the world's rarest gemstones, the finest specimens of alexandrite are costlier than diamonds - and its price understandably reflects its rarity. Discovered in the Ural Mountains of Russia in around 1830 on the birthday of Czar Alexander II and named after him, its key words are joy, wisdom and release of sorrow. A notable feature of this crystal is its stunning optical property of colour change - it is light red or red-purple in incandescent artificial light, and green (often an intense grass-green) or blue-green in daylight. Since green is the colour of new growth and pink the shade of impartial love, the Russian name for Alexandrite, 'Stone of Good Omen', could not be more apt.

This stone has a positive electrical charge which stays for hours after rubbing, and an energy factor which changes with its colour. But potent though this stone looks, it radiates sensitivity. In physical healing, it bypasses the actual condition and goes directly to the root of it and balances any disharmonies out. It is a regenerative stone, aiding the tissues of the body to renew after dis-ease - both internally and externally. It has even been used to treat leukaemia and cancer. These regenerative properties also extend to spiritual transformation and growth, enhancing your ability to find joy in life and aiding psychic protection when undertaking such work. It also carries the beneficial qualities of making one's head feel 'roomier', improving the memory, clearing the eyesight, and relieving any physical tensions. In its colour change, it signifies a spiritual metamorphosis and embodies an inner pattern of flexibility, adaptability and willingness to shift its expression in the presence of varying conditions; it can teach us this very quality in ourselves.

Since its discovery, alexandrite was believed to be a stone of good fortune in its native country. It carries a very joyful vibration and is a powerful agent of inner transformation and spiritual evolution. Primarily stimulating the Crown chakra, it embodies both the heart energy (green) and the higher mind energy (purple). It can stimulate a harmonic opening of the Heart, Third Eye and Crown chakras, during which the three can operate as an integrated whole. Alexandrite's emotional tone is one of exuberant joy. It calls forth the heart's natural state of delighted engagement and teaches us that the spiritual qualities of the celestial realms are also simultaneously here at every moment, encouraging us to take on all the energies that come to us and to do this with a pure commitment to joy. Overall, it centres, reinforces and realigns the mental, emotional and spiritual bodies, enhancing manifestation in all its forms. This precious, rare gem transmits inner peace by developing magnanimity of heart and should be valued and used extensively.

GEMINIAN POWER CRYSTALS

Around six thousand years ago, in ancient Mesopotamia, the Sumerians started studying precious stones and minerals, as well as the stars, with a view of improving their lives in many ways by probing the secrets and mysteries of the Universe. Their esoteric interests and knowledge were such that they began to grasp the general connections between the Earth and the heavens, or the Solar system as they knew it, and the functions of stones and minerals as a link between the two. Their method of making these connections was by colour (for example the Sun was allocated all yellow stones), as well as other spiritual links. The gemstones listed for the portion of your zodiac sign are given their status as your 'power crystals' due to the links that can be made between your primary planetary ruler/s and your mutable planetary ruler (listed last), and each stone's particular colour, chemical and mineral compositions, healing properties, and the number they are given (based on the Mohs scale of hardness: for example, diamond scores a perfect 10 out of 10), all of which combine to align with your planetary rulers. Working mindfully with your planet's special crystals is one way you can increase the flow of power and magic into your life.

POWER CRYSTALS FOR FIRST HALF GEMINIANS ★ (20 May - 4 June)

Influenced by Mercury and Venus

Padparadjah (Orange Sapphire), Taafeite, Moss Agate, Uvarovite, Staurolite, Verdite

★ **TAAFEITE** ★ Taafeite is one of the rarest and most desirable collector's crystals known. Only a few stones have ever been found. It comes in pink, mauve and violet. Discovered along with spinels by Count Charles Richard Taafe in 1945, Taafeite is almost as hard as a sapphire and about the same bodyweight. It was initially misidentified as a spinel, but the crucial difference lay in the fact that taafeite is doubly refractive while spinel is singly refractive. It is a brilliant, magical gem but, like the colourless sapphire, almost impossible to obtain. You might do well to make this your life's mission, knowing that if you do come across it, luck and good fortune have definitely smiled upon you.

★ **MOSS AGATE** ★ Moss agate has dark green and blackish green patterns imitative of ferns and moss against a creamy translucent or clear background. Moss agate, like all green stones, contains the energies of nature which are nurturing and balancing to the subtle energy systems. Green crystals can also promote feelings of freedom and space, and be used to release fear and remove 'tightness' that can become overwhelming when you feel trapped by inharmonious relationships or circumstances. Moss agate is often referred to as the 'gardener's stone', and is said to be helpful to farmers in ensuring a good crop by way of encouraging rain, abundance, fertility and protection of the Earth, and helping one communicate more effectively with animals and plants. Moss agate provides a link between the plant and mineral kingdoms, assisting in communicating with the natural world and nature spirits. It is also attributed to attracting and enhancing prosperity, success, healing, restoration, confidence, strength and creativity. Moss agate is a stabilising stone and is refreshing to the soul, helping you to see beauty in all you do or behold. As a stone of wealth, it also attracts abundance and encourages trust, optimism and hope in the Universe's gifts. Moss agate aligns with the Heart chakra and is a powerful mental and physical healer, working on emotional and thinking patterns that manifest dis-ease, helping to clear those patterns. Releasing fear and deep-rooted stress, it improves self-esteem and highlights positive personality traits. It is also believed that moss agate is beneficial when fostering new friendships or seeking a compatible lover.

★ **STAUROLITE** ★ Staurolite is usually a vibrant red or grey-brown stone, which derives its name from the Greek word *staurus*, meaning 'cross', as it is naturally cruciform. The Ancient Britons called these gems 'fairy stones' and used them in magical rites. The early Christians knew them as 'cross stones' and wore them as lucky charms, while myths speak of 'staurolite stars' falling from heaven. Staurolite today is known as the Fairy Cross and is traditionally a protective stone used as a talisman for good luck.

This stone is said to connect the physical, etheric and spiritual planes, promoting communication between them. As a Gemini power crystal, it is exceptionally useful at relieving nervous tension due to overwork or simply having too many things on the boil, as Airy folk are prone to do. Physically, staurolite provides a grounding energy for Airy souls also, and is especially useful for those wishing to give up smoking; as well as healing its ill-effects, it can assist in understanding the hidden reasons behind the nicotine addiction and will help heal the break between our past and future lifestyles - at those points where our spiritual life must meet with our material existence, staurolite smoothes over the cracks and aligns all levels of our being so we can feel more comfortable with any changes. The cross formation signifies the meeting of spirit and matter, death and rebirth, and so it is with our leaving behind our past as we move onto our higher spiritual destiny. Staurolite shows that the transition from darkness into light is easier than we think. Encouraging a less materially-based existence, it helps manifest only that which is needed to make our physical lives comfortable, and assists in rejecting that which does not benefit us spiritually.

POWER CRYSTALS FOR SECOND HALF GEMINIANS ★ (5 - 20 June)
Influenced by Mercury and Uranus

Cat's Eye, Chrysoberyl, Transvaal Jade, Grossular Garnet, Rubellite in Lepidolite, Geode (Potato Stone)

★ **CAT'S EYE** ★ The Greeks called this crystal 'Waving Light', but it is better known as cat's eye. This name applies because a single whitish line appears to move when the stone is held towards the light and rotated, resembling the contracted pupil of a cat's eye; this effect is known as chatoyancy. True cat's eye stones are made of a hard mineral called chrysoberyl. This especially valued, translucent gemstone may have a golden-yellow, bamboo-green or bluish-brown body, but whatever the tint, a powerful silver-white beam of light moves across its half-round or cabachon-cut surface when stimulated by movement. Known as the 'stone-gourmet's delight', this stone's main characteristic, a bright green ribbon of light, occurs through reflection of light from fine, parallelled fibres or hollow crystal tubes which the growing crystal encased when forming. Cat's eye has magical properties. It is a grounding stone, but is also effective at stimulating the intuitive functions. It is protective and dispels negative energy from the aura. The cat's eye has always been greatly valued in India, where it is regarded as a bringer of wealth - and a talisman to guard against the loss of wealth. A striking stone of beauty and playful magic, cat's eye is said to attract happiness, serenity, good fortune and luck. You may need that last quality, as cat's eye are generally regarded as the most beautiful of the 'ray' gems and priced accordingly.

★ **CHRYSOBERYL** ★ A stone of extreme hardness, chrysoberyl comes in hues of golden yellow, yellow with brown, and green with red. A form of beryl, chrysoberyl is a stone for new beginnings. Aligning the Solar Plexus and Crown chakras, it connects the mind and spirit and increases both personal and spiritual power. Chrysoberyl is an excellent stone for enhancing creativity, compassion, confidence, forgiveness and generosity. It strengthens self-worth and releases unhelpful or outworn energy patterns. Specific forms of chrysoberyl are alexandrite, cat's eye and cymophane (a type of cat's eye).

★ **GROSSULAR GARNET** ★ Grossular garnet, or grossularite, as well as having similar qualities to regular garnet, is usually an attractive reddish orange or brownish yellow stone. It is a useful stone to have during challenges and lawsuits, where courage or fortitude may be required. During such times of change or upheaval, it can provide a sense of grounding, calm and balance. It inspires service, cooperation, relaxation and 'going with the flow'. Garnet has an affinity for the Base and Sacral chakras, where it breaks down blockages and stimulates our untapped creative energy. It will also revitalise and balance energy in these chakras, bringing serenity or passion according to the need. Sometimes known as 'carbuncles' (when they are cut *en cabachon*, that is, flat at the bottom or with a convex rounded top instead of facets), garnets occur in many different shades, the most well-known being red. Garnet keeps us grounded, making us feel safe and secure. It can help lift melancholy and will help you find your inner strength and full potential by releasing your fear of failure. It assists in boosting confidence, imparting courage, building strength of character, and enabling us to find our inner strength and resources. It can help with any sexual difficulties, both mentally and physically, and is a stone of love and commitment which brings warmth, devotion, constancy, faithfulness, understanding, sincerity, trust and honesty to a relationship.

Innovative garnet encourages you to be more creative and stimulates the right brain, creating 'light-bulb' flashes of inspiration and thought. It is an energising and regenerative stone, especially for the two lowest bodily chakras, although it also works effectively on the Heart chakra. Garnet helps to dissolve unhelpful behavioural patterns and past hurts to allow you to become more self-empowered and move on. Further, if you are feeling impotent or stuck in plans that have not yet manifested, this stone assists in moving out of the stagnancy and into potent action. It is also useful in easing situations in which you feel trapped and there seems no way out, or where life has become chaotic or broken, offering hope in apparently hopeless circumstances. Garnet is a powerful attractor of abundance, and grossular garnet (or hexagonal green garnet) is an effective stone for creating a pentacle layout in magical workings. It is traditionally believed that wearing a square-cut garnet encourages success in business dealings. Garnet draws prosperity into your experience and offers support during challenges. It can also activate other crystals, amplifying their effect. It is interesting to note that skyscrapers built on New York's Manhattan Island have deep foundations driven into the island's bedrock, which contains a vast amount of garnet.

YOUR LUCKY NUMBERS

Your lucky numbers are ★ 3 for Gemini ^ & 5 for Mercury (also, see 'Lucky Magic Square of Mercury')

LUCKY MAGIC SQUARE OF MERCURY

In Western occult tradition, each planet has traditionally been associated with a series of numbers and particular arrangements of those numbers. One such method of numerological organisation is the magic square. Magic squares date back to ancient times, appearing in China about 3,000 years ago. The first Chinese square is seen in the scroll of the river Lo - the Lo-Shu, a scroll believed to have been created by Fuh-Hi, the mythical founder of Chinese civilisation. Certain squares came to be linked with the planets; these associations came from the Babylonians. Each *kamea*, or magic square, is linked with a particular planet, and each of the squares has a *seal*, which is the geometric pattern created by following the numbers in order of their value. This pattern touches upon all the numbers of the square and the seal is used to represent the entire square. An intelligence and a spirit are also associated with each kamea, derived from the key numbers contained within it, using a Hebrew form of numerology. This intelligence is viewed as an inspiring, guiding and informing entity.

The 'Magic Square of Mercury' is divided into 64 cells, or squares, eight across and eight down. The sum of the numbers in the vertical, horizontal and diagonal lines is a constant of 260. The total of these numbers is 2080. Therefore, the numbers 8, 64, 260 and 2080 are also assigned to Mercury.

YOUR NUMEROLOGY NUMBER & LUCKY SUN SIGN NUMBERS

"Everything that exists has a vibration. The vibration of sound, music, colour, matter, even our words, thoughts, and names show form. All vibration is measurable. To measure we need numbers. Numbers are the basis of all. Numbers are the key to all mysteries."
Shirley Blackwell Lawrence, *Behind Numerology*

Numerology is essentially the metaphysical * 'science' of numbers. The use of numbers in magic is its cornerstone of power. The ancient Greek philosopher and mathematician Pythagoras, born around 590 BC, embarked on a thirty-year spiritual quest studying with important religious and esoteric teachers and healers to find the mystery of 'The Hidden Light', and came to see mankind as living in three worlds: the natural, the human and the Divine. He asserted that all things can be expressed in numerical terms, because they are ultimately reducible to numbers. Pythagoras stated that "Numbers are the first things of all of Nature" and followed the theory that "Nothing can exist without numbers."

Many believe that numbers have an arcane, mystical relationship with words, and with inanimate and animate objects; the interpretations that arose from these relationships date back to a time when the dawning intelligence of primitive man first visualised the meaning of numbers and associated it with spiritual significance. Numerology is the science of the exploration of this relationship in order to discover hidden meanings, forecast the future or interpret the character of a person. In its more modern applications, a series of figures which correspond to an individual's name and date of birth are calculated, and practitioners believe one's prospects, fortune and character can be deciphered from the results ^.

So what is numerology and how does one use it? Everything in the Universe has a vibrational frequency, an energy, a force, all vibrating at various rates, and we as humans are no exception, the difference between one person and another is their rate of vibration. This force or energy is constantly in motion and changing, and we can even 'tune into' and feel our vibrations if we are still for long enough.

Along with letters, sounds, colours, crystals, and many other things, it is believed that numbers also have vibrations, and when we are able to familiarise ourselves with our own numerical frequencies, we can use this familiarity to add power and magic to our lives. The numbers of our birth date, the letters of our names, and the numbers of our Sun sign and ruling planets, all have a unique vibrational frequency, and herein lies the key to understanding our self and our journey through life. Numerology refers to the knowledge contained within the numbers of our birth date and our name, and this is our own personal magic which can greatly assist us through life.

* Metaphysics is the study of those sciences that extend beyond the physical or tangible

HOW TO FIND YOUR NUMEROLOGY NUMBER

^ Your Sun sign's number was added up according to the principle of corresponding a number with a letter, for example 1=A, 2=B, 3=C and so on in sequence and up to 9=I, then beginning again at number 1 for the next letter J and following this same sequence. Following this system, the sum of the letters in Gemini vibrates to the number 3.

Your personal numerology number is determined by adding up all the numbers in your birth date until they reach a two-digit figure. The two resulting numbers are then added together again to form a single digit, which is your personal numerology number. For example, someone born on 3 February 1983, would add the digits 3 + 2 + 1 + 9 + 8 + 3 = 26 = (reduced to two digits) 8. So that person's personal numerology birth number is 8.

Each primary number or birth number from 1 to 9 has a specific meaning and is governed by a planetary force. The principle of numerology reduces all numbers down to the following: 1 to 9, and 10, 11, 13 and 22 *. The last four numbers only apply to people specially concerned with the occult and spiritualism - and can be studied at greater length through other sources if so desired - and can in any case be reduced further to a single digit if preferred. Your birth number contains a unique power, and therein lie your strengths, shortcomings and opportunities. It is beyond the scope of this book to outline your individual numerology number possibilities, so for the purposes of astrological applications, I have only included your Sun sign and ruling planet's special numbers.

* The numbers 10 and 13, and the master numbers 11 and 22, can be further reduced to one digit if so desired; however, they can be interpreted as they are without further reduction. The choice is personal.

BASIC MEANINGS & KEYWORDS

1 ★ Sun. Masculine influence, beginnings, independence, inventiveness, originality, leadership, exploration, innovation, ambition
2 ★ Moon. Feminine influence, cooperation, partnership, tact, diplomacy, harmony, unity, emotions, imagination, adaptability
3 ★ Jupiter. Communication, expression, youthfulness, self-confidence, creativity, inspiration, optimism, curiosity
4 ★ Uranus. Order, form, security, stability, patience, restriction, work, values, practicality
5 ★ Mercury. Freedom, inconsistency, change, variety, travel, activity, learned
6 ★ Venus. Love, home, family, sense of duty, responsibility, marriage, justice, nurturing, balance, gentleness, peace, friendship
7 ★ Neptune. Analysis, wisdom, mystical, spiritual, solitude, precision, research, integrity, mystery, psychic perceptions

8 ★ Saturn. Money, power, success, organisation, hard work, business, health, purpose, control, authority, mastery

9 ★ Mars. Completion, endings, Universal, service, humanity, philanthropy, loyalty

10 ★ Fortunate, creative, vibrant, stable, optimistic, original, successful, determined, individualistic

11 ★ Master number. Prophecies, inspiration, moral courage, missionary, long-suffering, foolhardiness, enlightenment, invention

13 ★ Misunderstood, fearful, changeable, interested in the occult, fatalistic, flexible, sacred, beguiling

22 ★ Master number. Powerful, successful, idealistic, attracted to the occult, creative, wise, successful, masterful, spiritually understanding

★ THE NUMBER 5 - FOR MERCURY ★

Names ★ Quint, Quintuple, Pentad, Quinary, Quintet, and all names preceded with the prefix *pent*, from the Greek *pent* which means five: pentacle, pentagon, Pentecost, pentagram

Arithmomantic connections with the letters of the alphabet ★ E, N and W

Ruled by Mercury, this is a changeable number by nature. The number 5, symbolised by the five pointed star pentacle, is an intellectual vibration and is connected with freedom and movement, energy, travel and creativity. But the number 5 also represents unpredictability and instability, owing to the unstable and unbalanced nature of this number. This fickleness and uncertainty is associated with the number 5, as it carries no constant vibration and may change or shift. The quincunx, the number 5, or the Pentad, was regarded by the followers of Pythagoras, as well as other philosophers, as the symbol of health and prosperity, but on the whole it seems universally to have symbolised marriage, fecundity and propagation, this belief probably having its origin in the idea of 5 being the union of 3 and 2, or a male and female number (in Ancient Rome, its significance was emphasised by the burning of 5 tapers during the marriage ceremony). A fifth element indeed exists, and was described by Plutarch in the 1st century AD, in these words: "If we assume that the World in which we live is the only one there is ... then it is itself made up of, as it were, five worlds which make Harmony of it: one is the Earth, another Water, the third Fire, the fourth Air, and the fifth Sky, with the last one being called Light by some and Ether by others and by yet others, Quintessence." It could be said that 5 is the number of transformation, representing the combination of the four elements plus spirit (or ether). The magical symbol of the five-pointed star is an Egyptian hieroglyph for the womb, as well as one form of the ancient Seal of Solomon. Five is associated with magical gateways, and indicates that there may be challenges ahead, but these will help you develop your skills. Five - the number of the physical senses - symbolises the planet Mercury, and people born under this number are mercurial in temperament and characteristics.

It is a quixotic number of quicksilver temperament and ideas, and signifies communication, an artistic streak and extreme creativity. Number 5s are the ideas people, who hate being tied down to anything resembling a routine or time schedule. Carrying the Mercurial vibe, this is the number of adventure and communication which embodies the concept of "variety is the spice of life." People under its influence will likely have many irons burning on as many different fires as possible at the same time. It can also indicate travel and movement so is perfect for all those with wanderlust and who welcome the world and new experiences with open arms. You are the great communicators of life and love to travel far afield, making excellent explorers and adventurers. It can be contrary and irresponsible, however it is often the number associated with fame and notoriety. Commitment can be a big problem for 5s, because there is so much out there to investigate. You may also be chaotic, uncommitted, inconsistent, self-indulgent, unstable, careless, and attracted to immoral or unvirtuous activities. You are energetic, lively, impulsive, adventurous, daring, freedom-loving, versatile, curious, adaptable, sociable, flexible, sensual, quick-thinking, romantic, fun-loving, accommodating, witty, courageous and worldly, but may be highly strung and have trouble with your nerves. You are good at making money, especially by risk or speculation, and you bounce back easily from any setback. You make friends easily with people born under any other number, but close friends will probably be fellow number 5s. Wednesday is the luckiest day for the quicksilver number 5.

Alchemy ★ Five stands for dynamic focus, a combination of two and three. It can be sparkling, sexual or charismatic, or on the other hand, a decisive act of destruction. It can also represent the quintessential element which is a distillation of all four basic elements. A five-pointed star, the pentagram (five points joined by one line) or a pentagon (a five-sided figure) are its main representations.

LUCKY 'MAGIC HOURS' OR 'TIME UNITS'

One rule of magic, luck and power, as already outlined elsewhere in this book, can be found within the well-known phrase, "As above, so below." From the most ancient times, the planets were said to rule Earthly destinies and powers. Days of the week were named after the seven planets which were the only ones then known: Sun Day, Moon Day, Mars Day (French: Mardi), Mercury Day (French: Mercredi), Jove Day (French: Jeudi), Venus Day (French: Vendredi) and Saturn Day.

The planetary hours are based on an ancient astrological system, the Chaldean order of the planets. The Chaldean order indicates the relative orbital velocity of the planets, and from a heliocentric (helios = The Sun) perspective, this sequence also indicates the relative distance of the planets from the Sun (the Sun switching places with the Earth in this sequence), and the distance of the Moon from the Earth.

Before an action is taken in daily life, or a transaction undertaken, for instance, it is possible to choose the appropriate day and hour that will provide the greatest chances of success. By studying the planetary hours system, you will discover which actions are propitious to which of the seven planets or 'star-gods' and at what time it would be advisable to undertake them.

The planetary hours system uses this Chaldean order to divide time, and each planetary hour of the planetary day is ruled by a different planet. The order is repeated, starting with the slowest: Saturn - then, Jupiter, Mars, Sun, Venus, Mercury, Moon, then back to Saturn, Jupiter, Mars, etc, ad infinitum. The planet that rules the first hour of the day is also the ruler of that whole day and gives the day its name. So the first hour of Saturday is ruled by Saturn, the first hour of Sunday by the Sun, and so on. It is important, for the purposes of using specific planetary energies for our magic and wishes, to note that planetary hours are not considered the same length as our normal time-keeping slots of sixty minutes. Each day is split into time periods, day time and night time, beginning at around sunrise and sunset respectively. These two time periods are each divided into twelve equal-length hours, which are the planetary hours. So the planetary hours of the day and the planetary hours of the night will be of different lengths, except during the equinoxes when light and darkness are balanced.

In sequence, the Sun, Moon and the five visible planets each exerts its own special influence over a twenty-four-hour period. I like to call your planet's special day and hour the 'Magic Hour'.

Magic rituals to draw luck and love to you should be conducted at astrologically correct times and with the appropriate instruments, tools, cards, herbs, flowers, oils and plants which are linked with the ruling planet. For example, a love ritual, spell or potion demands a concoction of any or all of the above ruled by Venus. Do not underestimate rulerships, for they wield an unseen power that can help make our dreams, big and small, come true.

Further, as specific hours of each day are ruled by certain planets, if you are really serious about attracting some power, luck or magic into your life, it is imperative that you wish, pray or ask at the most opportune times for your Sun sign. There are two methods you can use for fine tuning your magical workings. The first method is to perform your spell, ritual or wishing on the day your Sun sign's ruling planet during the planetary hour that signifies the essence of what you are asking for (e.g. An Arien who is looking for love might perform a love-seeking ritual on a Tuesday, during a Venus-ruled planetary hour). Alternatively, if you wish to summon the power of your Sun sign's own ruling planet, then that same Arien might perform their love-seeking ritual on a Friday (ruled by Venus) during Mars's planetary hour.

The nature of that which you are asking for, such as love, travel opportunities, money, career guidance, protection or friendship for example, should always be considered when choosing the day or hour during which your magic will be heightened.

The answer to the question why are there seven days in a week, is a very important one to know in unravelling the secret of your Magic Hours. Ancient people recognised the supreme importance of the seven heavenly spheres, which comprised those which could be seen by the naked eye: the Sun, Moon, Mercury, Venus, Mars, Jupiter and Saturn. They then named each of the seven days of the week after one of those spheres and assigned that planetary 'ruler' to one day of the week. As viewed from Earth, these seven spheres appear to move at varying speeds, and the ancients used this factor to arrange them in order of varying speed. If you intend to use your Magic Hours to attract wonderful things, you must memorise that sequence because it is what forms the basis of the whole system.

Whenever you intend to use your Magic Hours or, perhaps more accurately, Magic *Time Units*, it is important to find out the exact time of sunrise for the area in which you live, as sunrise marks the time when your planet's magic is at its most powerful on its specific day. So, at sunrise on Sunday, the Sun rules the hour following the sunrise, the Moon rules the first hour following sunrise on a Monday, and through the week the pattern is repeated, with each day's ruling planet beginning the cycle in that first hour after dawn. It is logical then, that the rest of the planets, in sequence, follow on with one planet per hour for that day thereafter for the rest of the 24-hour cycle, creating a Magic Hour or Time Unit for each planet throughout the day and night, depending on which planet rules that particular day and is therefore the first in line.

If you wish to explore the idea in more depth, it is worth noting first and foremost that each day contains twenty-four hours, but, depending on the season, day and night will be of varying lengths. In summer, daylight is longer than darkness, whereas the reverse applies in winter. During autumn and spring, day and night are usually about equal. Therefore, although a complete day always contains twenty-four hours, there are not always twelve hours between sunrise and sunset and another twelve hours between sundown and the following sunrise. So, depending on the season (and location), a time unit may be shorter than one hour, longer than one hour, or equal to one hour. So whenever you intend to use your Magic Time Units, it is important to find out the exact time of sunrise and sunset for the area in which you live. The next step is to divide the amount of day time (if day when you wish to work your 'magic', otherwise the same following theory applies to night time) into twelve equal sections by calculating the number of hours and minutes between sunrise and sunset and divide by twelve. An example is if the Sun rises at 6.27 a.m. and sets at 5.49 p.m., the amount of time contained in this day is eleven hours and twenty-two minutes. Convert this total into minutes (682) and then divide that figure by twelve (57). Therefore, each of the twelve daylight time units will be 57 minutes on that day.

Although this wonderful method of using astrology is very ancient, it may be completely new to you. You are in for a pleasant surprise though, because if you are willing to delve into a little research and put the system to the test, rich rewards are in store for you!

YOUR LUCKY DAY ★ WEDNESDAY

Planet ★ Mercury
Basic Energy ★ Speed
Basic Magic ★ Communication, Study, Information
Element ★ Air
Colours ★ Blue, Yellow or Silver
Energy Keywords ★ Expression, Activity, Communication, Siblings, Dexterity, Adaptability, Intelligence, Agility, Versatility, Analysis, Verbosity, Restlessness, Neighbours, Awareness, Articulation, Brilliance, Changeability, Efficiency, Discrimination, Precision, Reason

Wednesday is the day of Mercury, your planetary ruler. In commonly used calendars, Wednesday is the fourth day of the week, though in others it is the third. The English name is derived from Old English *Wodnesdaeg*, and Middle English *Wednesdei*, meaning 'Day of Woden' or a claque of the Latin *dies Mercurii*, or 'Day of Mercury'. The god Woden was interpreted in the Roman era as the Germanic Mercury. Ash Wednesday, the first day of Lent in the Western Christian tradition, is perhaps the most well-known day with which Mercury's day is associated.

In the folk rhyme 'Monday's Child', 'Wednesday's child is full of woe'. Wednesday is the time for Mercury's powers of communication, to link up with long-lost friends, to communicate with a passed over loved one, or write important correspondences. It is also an opportune day to ask for qualities such as versatility, agility, articulate expression, reason, wit, humour, adaptability, intellectuality, and overall efficiency - as all are themes of Mercury. Mercury or Hermes is the god of thieves, so if something has been stolen from you, now could be the time to ask for it back in some form or another.

MERCURY'S MAGIC TIME UNITS
(BASED ON THE PLANETARY HOURS
FOR EACH DAY OF THE WEEK)

SATURDAY ★ Sixth time unit after sunrise
SUNDAY ★ Third and Tenth time units after sunrise
MONDAY ★ Seventh time unit after sunrise
TUESDAY ★ Fourth and Eleventh units after sunrise
WEDNESDAY ★ First and Eighth time units after sunrise
THURSDAY ★ Fifth and Twelfth time units after sunrise
FRIDAY ★ Second and Ninth time units after sunrise **

Choose the Hour/s of Mercury for any transaction, initiative, exchange, activity or venture which involves communication, siblings, your neighbours or neighbourhood, education, writing, service, social gatherings, intellectual pursuits, pets, information-gathering and research, and short journeys.

** Please note that for the purposes of simplification, the information regarding 'Mercury's Magic Time Units' is a very diluted and simplified version of using magical times to your advantage. These hours cover only daylight hours, or the first twelve hours after sunrise, and do not take into account magical times after sunset or throughout the night. 'Hours' is also a deceptive term, as most 'time periods' used in this system are less than an hour, but for the purposes of simplifying the technique, I refer to them as Magic Hours (to keep with the tradition of the term 'planetary hours') rather than magic 'time units', which is what they really are. Should you wish to do further research on your ruling planet's most powerful time units, or require further information about the planet/s from which you are seeking 'energy' from in order to assist your wish-making, other sources may provide you with more comprehensive and detailed information.

A LITTLE NEW MOON / MAGICAL TIME UNIT WISH RITUAL

Step 1 ~ Choose the Magical Hour and/or day that matches your intentions. The first dawn hour of Sunday, ruled by the Sun, is a great time for all-purpose magic, success, joy, abundance, prosperity, bliss, personal power & all-round expansion.

Step 2 ~ Write out a little wish list with the appropriate coloured pen on the colour paper which corresponds to your desire.

Step 3 ~ Choose a small stone of your choosing that is connected to your wish (or a number of stones that are perhaps linked with your planetary ruler's number, for example 5 for Mercury).

Step 4 ~ Find a nice patch of soil in your garden or any special place to you, dig into it, affirm your wish in your mind, place the crystal/s and piece of paper in the hole, then place a plant on top of the crystal/s and wish list.

Step 5 ~ Fill the soil back in over the roots of the plant and feed it with a little water out of a magical vessel (a small genie bottle would be ideal).

Step 6 ~ Thank the Earth, the Universe and the Sun (or whatever planet you are summoning the power from) for bringing forth your desires.

Step 7 ~ Repeat all day long: "Thank You, Thank You, Thank You!"

Step 8 ~ Watch your plant - and your wish - grow bigger and bigger as time goes on!

YOUR LUCKY CHARM/TALISMANS

The following are three 'materials' or talismanic symbols from which to make your lucky charms, and the planetary energy under which to do it, corresponding with your Sun sign:

GEMINI ★ Agate, Caduceus, Silver, Mercury

"When any star ascends fortunately, take a stone and
herb that are under that star, make a ring of
the metal that is congruous therewith, and in that fix
the stone with the herb under it."
Henry Cornelius Agrippa, *On Occult Philosophy*

Charms, talismans and amulets are among the oldest forms of magic. A charm or talisman is a symbol, often used to communicate a thought, prayer or wish to, or to make a connection with the Divine. It is usually in the form of an object, which has been imbued with mysterious and magical powers. A charm may be as simple as a stone, a flower or a feather, or it might be a parchment bearing writing; the meaning and significance that you attribute to the symbol is what is important. It can be created by yourself (to best effect) or by someone else, and works as a tool to activate our subconscious mind.

You can use general charms such as a cross, or a universally lucky symbol such as a horseshoe, but you will exude and therefore attract more potency and protection if you make and wear the appropriate charms with the matching gemstone, set in the right metal and created under the corresponding planetary influence. While most people wear silver or gold, cheaper tin or copper may be more appropriate and indeed beneficial for your Sun sign. An amulet (for protection) or a talisman or charm (for luck), must also be made, ordered, designed or purchased on the appropriate day of the week for its power to be most effective. Your day, as previously described, is Wednesday.

You can even go further and create or buy your amulet or charm at one of the hours and/or days when your planet is exerting it's most powerful influence. It may sound complicated and requiring of forethought and effort, but if you are going to summon magic and are superstitious enough to truly *believe* that you can do this (and remember pure belief in something is the starting point of all manifestation), you should be scrupulous enough to do it properly. For your planet's day and time, please consult the information under the previous headings 'Your Lucky Day' and 'Mercury's Magic Time Units'.

GODS, GODDESSES, ANIMAL TOTEMS & OTHER 'GUIDES'

Gods, goddesses and guides can be summoned to help you live your life to its optimal best. Some are connected with your Sun sign, while others may be of your own personal choosing, ones you may feel particularly drawn towards. Those which align with your ruling planet and your Sun sign, give a good indication of those who will shine a guiding light along your desired path, but you can choose your own too, based upon exploration, observations, research, meditation or simple intuition - I believe choosing your own, based on your inner *knowing* or guidance system, is a very powerful magical tool. However, to get you started, following are some animal spirit guide ideas for your contemplation. Good luck!

YOUR LUCKY ANIMALS & BIRDS

Dog, Monkey, Beetles, Small Birds, Weasel, Parrot, Squirrel, Magpie, Greyhound, Hyena, Apes, Linnet, Butterfly, Serpent, Spider, Eagle, Fox, Bee, Finch, Deer

"Somewhere beyond the walls of our awareness … the wilderness side, the hunter side, the seeking side of ourselves is waiting to return."
Laurens van der Post, *The Heart of the Hunter*

"(People) everywhere are being made acutely aware of the fact that something essentially to life and wellbeing is flickering very low in the human species and threatening to go out entirely. This 'something' has to do with such values as love, unselfishness, sincerity, loyalty to one's best friend, honesty, enthusiasm, humility, goodness, happiness … fun. Practically every animal has these assets in abundance and is eager to share them, given the opportunity and the encouragement."
Jay Allen Boone, *Kinship with All Life*

Some astrological systems, such as Shamanistic * or Native American Astrology, tell us that the Sun sign we were born under has a corresponding animal totem, which informs us about our characteristics and act as a kind of spiritual guide or mentor throughout our life's journey. These totems are described as Solar totems, because many of them share similarities with the Solar system and the sign the Sun was passing through at the time of our birth, and therefore relate to animals and animal behaviours which also correspond to environmental conditions and seasonal changes. These animals encompass many aspects of the Solar system, from seasonal relationships, to creature instincts, to reciprocal links with the planetary vibrations, and 'clans' within nature that you are inherently closely connected with through your date of birth.

Carl Jung, a master of dream analysis and interpretation, proposed that animals symbolise our natural instincts, operating through our dreams. He theorised that certain dream symbols, among them animals, represent core emotions and concepts, archetypes that will hold true for all of us the world over, regardless of so-called 'divisions' such as sex, customs, age or culture. In *Man and His Symbols*, Jung states that primitive societies believed that each person had a bush soul and a human soul. The bush soul incarnates as a tree or animal - a totem - and when the bush soul is harmed or injured, the human soul is considered injured as well.

Some of the most important and powerful spirit guides are those belonging to the animal kingdom. Both in ancient times and in some traditional modern tribal systems, people consult with animals for their wisdom and personal power. Even though most societies today have drifted away from this connection, it has never really left us, and different creatures continue to communicate with us on both the physical and spiritual planes in an attempt to speak to our souls and spirits.

As part of the teaching world, animals can bring us wisdom and survival skills, while others show us how to adapt, transcend or morph. Others still can remind us the importance of play and humour, and guide us around how to overcome life's challenges. Many are known for their loyalty and ability to love unconditionally and without judgement, while some have a grounded and healthy detachment, remaining true to themselves rather than pleasing others, an important lesson in itself. Whatever the qualities of the unique animal guides for your Sun sign, all have some enlightening soul-awakening traits that can teach us much about our own true inner selves. Ultimately, your animal spirit guides, and in particular your Solar totem animal, endow you with qualities that will enhance your life and help to activate your creativity, wisdom and intuition, helping to heal the broken or return the lost pieces of your soul and reconnect you to the natural world.

Your Solar totem animal (listed last on your lucky birds and animals list) is not the same as an animal spirit guide, which is based on metaphysical principles and is also based on your soul's mission in this embodiment - however, you can definitely make your birth Solar totem animal your spiritual guide if you wish, as you may find that its qualities, traits, symbolism and messages strongly reflect and define your own nature - or what you aspire to become, manifest or draw towards you. Your birth totem power animal comes from a place of trust and innocence, and represents the essence of your creative inner child. If you spend some time meditating on your Solar totem animal, asking what lessons it can teach, and reflect deeply on its character, life and habits, you may find it connects with you on a deep spiritual level and you can make the necessary changes to your life to draw in more magic and power.

Overall, if your life is stagnant or in need of healing or an energy boost, you can request your animal spirit or spirits to come and help you change your vibration, awaken your truth and arouse your inner forces. If you are aware of your animal spirit's presence in your life every day, you can use its particular energies to support, guide and teach you. And above all, pay attention to any signs and expressions of its lessons, and remember to thank your chosen animal guide for helping you.

* Shamanism is a traditional spiritual practice of the Native American culture. A shaman, one who practices this age-old art, is an intermediary between the human world and the world of the spirits. He inherits his magical powers at birth, but spends many years as an apprentice, so that he is usually much older in age before he is able to practice and call upon his skills. People ask for a shaman's help when there is a crisis on either a personal or wider spread scale, such as famine, drought, war or illness. The shaman makes contact with the spirits by going into a trance. First, he may perform a series of rituals, which usually include drumming, singing and chanting, and when these have brought on the right conditions, he leaves his body behind to travel to the other world. There he meets with the spirits of his ancestors, who inform him what must be done to relieve the suffering of his people. If the shaman is asked to cure someone of a dis-ease, then the spirits may accompany him to find the correct medicinal herbs or treatments for his patient.

YOUR FEATURE ANIMAL ★ DEER

The Deer's Message ★ Be gentle in word, thought and touch
Brings the totem gift of ★ Sociability, inspiration, lively conversation, majesty, compassion
Shares the power energies of ★ A youthful outlook, unique humour, clear expression, gentleness
Brings forth and teaches the magic of ★ Grace, respectability, charm, daintiness

As well as being a Universal symbol of dainty grace, the Deer also represents unconditional love and kindness. Deer medicine teaches us the ability to listen, to express gratitude and to understand what is necessary for survival. As your totem animal, she can also impart the wisdom of connecting to the woodlands goddess, sacrificing for the higher good, and alternative paths to a goal.

The muse of the Solar totem animals, the Deer is inspiring, lively and quick-witted. Possessing a unique brand of humour, the Deer can raise a laugh out of almost anyone. With an excellent capacity for verbal expression and communication, the Deer is naturally intelligent and a consummate conversationalist. Ever alert to her surroundings, and always aware of her appearance, she can be a little self-consumed and narcissistic, but these traits are usually forgiven due to her natural congeniality and affability. She can be selfish, moody, lazy, impatient and two-faced, however her natural charm will overcome most shortcomings. The Deer's natural effervescence and sparkling wit can shine even brighter in a supportive environment, and she is an inspiring force that radiates love and energy when in a nurturing relationship.

The Deer brings healing through the power of love and gentleness. Treading softly and daintily, this subtle animal has the ability to appear and disappear in the wink of an eye.

In the Celtic tradition, the Deer embodies two aspects - male and female. The female Deer symbolises femininity, grace and subtlety. She is believed to call us from the Faery realm, helping us to release the material trappings of civilisation, and to delve deep into the forest's treasure to explore our magical and spiritual selves. The male Deer, the Stag, is also linked to the sacredness of the magical woods, representing independence, pride and purification. It is believed the set of antlers growing from the male's head are antennae which connect it to higher energy sources. If you come across one in the wild and it is your power animal, try to count the number of points on their antlers, as this number is said to have numerological significance for you.

The Stag brings the qualities of integrity and dignity into our lives. A majestic and graceful animal associated with the Horned God of Western Paganism, the Stag symbolises fatherhood and teaches us the authority of grace and wisdom over aggression and force. It helps to know your own strength and how to best use it. The Stag is lord of the forest and protector of its creatures, and will help advise you on how to stay true to yourself and remain respectable.

The Deer's senses are very acute and they can see extremely well in low light, giving them the ability to understand the deeper meaning of things. From a great distance, they can hear a twig snap, and are well-known for this alertness and necessary swiftness of foot. They are also intuitive, often seeming to possess extrasensory perceptions, and anyone with this as their power animal is likely to possess equally sharp, if latent, clairvoyant and clairaudient abilities. You can see between the shadows, detect sudden movements, catch fleeting glimpses, and 'hear' that which isn't making audible noise - the Deer can indeed help you to develop these qualities further.

The Deer teaches us to be gentle above all else, and to have compassion for, to protect and to touch the hearts and minds of wounded beings in our lives, by gently nudging them in the right direction rather than forcing them to change. The love that comes from Deer medicine teaches us to love and accept others for who or what they are, and that true power lays in softness and compassion. Ultimately they teach us how powerful - and empowering - it is to be of gentle demeanour, and to exert keen observation and sensitivity. Sacred carriers of peace, they are in tune with nature and all it comprises, with an unconditional and unassuming acceptance of it. With the Deer as your totem, your life is sure to abound with opportunities to express that gentle love that will open doors for you everywhere.

SPIRITUAL KEEPER ★ EAGLE

Your spiritual keeper guides your spiritual growth and brings illumination. Your spiritual keeper is determined by the season in which you were born. Regarded as the 'keepers' or 'caretakers' of the Universe, the four Directions or alignments were also referred to by the Native Americans as the Four Winds because their presence was *felt* rather than seen. The Direction to which your birth time belongs influences the nature of your inner senses. The East Direction's totem is the Eagle.

The Eagle is a symbol of freedom, victory and spirit. It flies higher than any other bird, high enough to 'touch the Sun'. The golden Eagle is a symbol of peace, and an Eagle flying overhead is a sign of Shaman power, sometimes taken as a call to that vocation. To the shaman, the Eagle is a messenger, bringing instructions from the spirit of the night. As Halifax states, "When shamans get power, it always comes from the night." The Eagle is the sacred messenger, flying high to carry our prayers to the Great Spirit and returning with gifts of illumination and clear vision. The Eagle enables us to see the bigger picture, to rise above our Earthly concerns, and reminds us to pay attention to the things that really matter in life. This majestic bird brings you the totem gift of freedom, mission and perfect timing, sharing the power energies and magic of pride, spirit and manifestation. Your animal keeper the Eagle is, above all, a potent symbol of vision and strength.

CLAN ★ BUTTERFLY

Your clan animal comes from a place of inner knowing and intuition, helping you to discover the essence and magic of your true self. The Butterfly, a totem of the Air clan, represents and protects all that is beautiful and holds the secrets of change and personal transformation. The Butterfly symbolises that this transformation is always available to you, and may even begin without your conscious participation. Butterfly *is* the power of Air, the ability to float along on a breeze, and to 'dance' from place to place. They awaken our sense of lightness and joy, and teach us to dance with life rather than take it too seriously.

In the folklore of some tribes, butterflies stand for change and balance, while in others ephemeral beauty, and some believe it to be symbolic of vanity and frivolity. Many tribes consider butterflies to be symbols of good luck, and some associate them with sleep and dreaming, decorating cradleboards and other children's items to help induce calm sleep and bring pleasant dreams. Butterflies symbolise metamorphosis, teaching us to trust in the process of change, re-awaken us to joy, and teach us that life is full of surprises and to therefore live with a constant sense of passion, intensity and wonder.

YOUR CORRESPONDING CHINESE ASTROLOGY ANIMAL

The Chinese Zodiac, known as Sheng Xiao (literally meaning 'birth likeness'), is based on a twelve-year cycle, each year in that cycle related to a particular animal. These animals are: Rat, Ox, Tiger, Rabbit, Dragon, Snake, Horse, Sheep, Monkey, Rooster, Dog and Pig. The selection and order of the animals that so influence people's lives, particularly in East Asian cultures, originated in the Han Dynasty (202 BC - 220 AD) and was based upon each animal's traits, characteristics, tendencies and living habits. Further, ancient people observed that there were twelve Full Moons in a year, and that, among other similarly related celestial observations, suggests its origins are also based on astronomical concepts.

The legend of the Chinese zodiac's story usually begins with the Jade Emperor, or Buddha (depending on who is telling the tale), summoning all the animals of the Universe for a race or a banquet. The twelve animals of the zodiac all appeared at the palace, and the order in which they arrived determined the order of the Chinese zodiac.

Each oriental animal corresponds with a Western astrology sign. For Gemini, it is the Horse.

"I am the Kaleidoscope of the mind.
I impart light, colour and perpetual motion.
I think, I see, I am moved by electric fluidity.
Constant only in my inconstancy
I am shackled by mundane holds,

> Unchecked by sturdy, binding goals.
> I run unimpeded through virgin paths.
> My spirit unconquered -
> My soul forever free.
> *I am the Horse."*
> **Theodora Lau**

Chinese name for the Horse ★ MA
Ranking Order ★ Seventh
Hours ruled by the Horse ★ 11 a.m. to 1 p.m.
Direction ★ Directly South
Season and principle month ★ Summer - June
Corresponds to the Western sign ★ Gemini

★ **HORSE** ★ *Fixed Element Fire*

★ **Keywords** ★

Hardworking, popular, witty, vital, independent, active, sociable, intelligent, talented, perceptive, selfish, fickle, impatient

The Horse is the seventh animal of the Chinese horoscope. Traditionally a yang sign, the Horse is romantic, successful and sensual. They fall in love quickly but are fickle in romance, and are reputed to change lovers a lot more frequently than the other signs. Active and energetic, Horse types exude sex-appeal like no other. In general, the Horse is regarded as gifted, but the truth is that it is more cunning than intelligent. Rebellious and boundlessly ambitious, the Horse can be hot-headed, hot-blooded and impatient. Their characters are full of contradictions and paradoxes - they will give up everything for love, yet lose interest quickly; they are proud yet sweet-natured; envious but tolerant; arrogant yet oddly modest; conceited yet humble; they want to belong, yet crave independence; they desire love and intimacy, yet dislike being cornered. Above all, perhaps the Horse type is just like the creature itself: born to run wild and as free as the wind.

YOUR METALS

Geminian power metals are Quicksilver (Mercury), Chrome and Zinc

Although the magic power of crystals is widely recognised and applied, the influence radiating from metals is often overlooked. Metal, too, emits a powerful energy and in fact, in Chinese philosophy, metal is considered so essential and powerful that it is classified as one of the elements, alongside Air, Fire, Earth and Water.

As already mentioned earlier in the book, throughout the writings of early philosophers and theorists, there are countless references to the unmistakable mystic connection between the seven known planets of the time, and Earthly affairs, ailments and objects. Seven metals were connected with the seven planets, to which seven colours and the seven 'transformations' were added. So the ancient alchemist came to share the astrological doctrine that each planet ruled a mineral: the Sun ruled gold, the Moon silver, Mars iron, Venus copper, Saturn lead, Jupiter tin, and Mercury quicksilver. Consequently, in alchemical symbolism the same sign came to represent the nominated metal and its corresponding planet.

QUICKSILVER

Quicksilver, also known as mercury, is a chemical element with symbol Hg, is heavy and as its name suggests, is silvery in colour. A mysterious, much-maligned and paradoxical metal, although its surface reflects light like shiny polished steel, the fluidity of this substance does not allow it to maintain any shape. Mercury is nearly 14 times as heavy as water, its density meaning that heavier things can easily float on top of it. But like water, it evaporates, albeit much more slowly, and in the air it is much more noxious and dangerous than in its liquid state.

Mercury is an extremely rare element in the Earth's crust, and many former mines which produced a large proportion of the world supply, have now been completely mined out. Today China is the top producer of mercury, but because of the high toxicity of this element, the mining of cinnabar (the mineral from which it is mostly extracted) and the refining of it for mercury, are hazardous and can produce serious health effects through mercury poisoning.

Quicksilver is the only metallic element that is liquid at standard conditions for temperature and pressure. It is perhaps best - and menacingly - known as a toxin - and indeed, mercury poisoning can result from water-soluble forms of quicksilver, inhalation of its vapour, or eating seafood contaminated with it. Some countries have banned the use of mercury in all products and production methods, while many others agreed in the Minamata Convention on Mercury, to prevent emissions.

Because it is liquid like water and shiny like silver, mercury's name was derived from the word *hydrargyrum* (where the chemical symbol Hg comes from), a Latinised form of the Greek word *hydra-gyros*, meaning 'water-silver'. The element itself was named after the Roman god Mercury, known for his speed and mobility.

Found in Ancient Egyptian tombs that date from 1500 BC, in China and Tibet, mercury use was thought to prolong life, heal fractures and generally promote overall wellbeing and health (although it is now known that exposure to mercury vapour can lead to serious adverse health effects.)

Its use in alchemy was widespread. Alchemists thought of Mercury as the First Matter from which all metals were formed, believing that different metals could be produced by varying the quality and quantity of sulphur contained within the mercury, the purest of these being gold. Mercury was therefore summoned in attempts to transmute the base (impure) metals into gold, which was the ultimate goal of many alchemists. This quest left a lasting legacy: the Sanskrit word for alchemy is *Rasavatam*, which means 'the way of mercury'; and mercury is the only metal for which the alchemical planetary name became the common name.

Used in thermometers and other measuring equipment, float valves, vermilion paint pigment, fluorescent lamps, mercury switches and other devices, mercury is also used in industrial chemicals, for electrical and electronic applications, as an ingredient in dental amalgams, in some batteries, as a preservative in vaccines, and as a compound in some over-the-counter drugs, as well as some niche uses including skin tanner vapour lamps, 'neon lights' and some cosmetic mascaras.

Natural sources, such as volcanoes, account for approximately half of all atmospheric mercury emissions, but the human-generated half can be divided into estimated percentages, the highest of these emissions (around 65 per cent and around 11 per cent) said to come from coal-fired power plants and gold production respectively.

Despite its well-known dangers and sinister reputation as a toxic heavy metal, an increasing amount of quicksilver is being used as gaseous mercury in fluorescent lamps, and it is still used in some thermometers, especially those which are used to measure high temperatures. However most of its other uses and applications are being gradually phased out due to health and safety regulations, and are being replaced with less toxic but considerably more expensive alternatives.

* Mercury and most of its compounds are extremely toxic and must be handled with care, if at all. Mercury can be absorbed through the skin and mucous membranes and mercury vapours can be inhaled. The most toxic forms of mercury are its organic compounds, which can cause both acute and chronic poisoning. Pregnant women should avoid this metallic element at all costs, particularly by avoiding eating large species of fish and all varieties of shellfish, as ingested mercury is considered an accumulative neurotoxin that can adversely affect the unborn foetus in numerous ways.

PLANTS, HERBS, SPICES, TREES, SHRUBS, FLOWERS, SCENTS & INCENSE

Plants have long been associated with magic, medicinal properties, superstition, nutrition and even astrology. In ancient times, some were endowed with magical properties based upon beliefs of the time, but also upon anecdotal evidence that some herbal concoctions, flowers or essences helped alleviate and even cure uncomfortable, painful or dis-eased physical or mental states. Whether these were based upon 'old wives tales' or beliefs in supernatural forces matters little, for in modern times we can prove and indeed *have* proven through scientific research and controlled experiments, that plants have their place in our health and medicine cabinets. Some 'magical' plants have aphrodisiac or narcotic properties, while others have formidable toxic effects, but all are considered in some way to affect the human system on physical, spiritual and psychological levels. Plants such as cocoa, tobacco and coffee, which have accompanied humans over the course of millennia, are still, more than ever, an integral part of our daily lives. They still incite the same pleasures, the same fascinations, and the same dangers, and some still carry the same taboos. It is interesting to note that more than 80 per cent of chemical medicines in existence today, and found in pharmacists' dispensaries, are made from plants.

In modern astrology herbs are often associated with the zodiac signs and have evolved from an old system where a specific planet rules each herb. The planet that governs an herb is chosen according to its appearance, scent and where it grows; herbs are additionally categorised as hot or cold, and dry or moist. In this way you can see how the nature of the herb corresponds to the nature of the planet. If you are familiar with your ruling planets' basic associations, you will find it easy to match it to herbs. Although you can simply buy whatever herbs you wish to use for your magic, the optimum effect will be obtained if you can gather them at a favourable astrological time. Once you are armed with astrological knowledge, you can choose a time when the planet that rules your chosen herb is in a position of strength. Keep in mind that each planet rules a substantial amount of plants, so if one isn't easily obtained, it should be simply to find another one to use for the same purpose.

There sometimes seems to be a wide variance in the list of herbs associated with a specific astrological influence. This is because the different parts of the plant have different rulerships and uses. For example, whichever planet rules it, a plant that bears fruit is naturally related to Jupiter, its flowers relate to Venus, seed or bark to Mercury, leaves to the Moon, wood to Mars, and roots to Saturn. So, as well as the planet that traditionally rules the plant, it can be regarded as having a secondary ruler according to the part of the plant being used. Although you don't need to work with a highly complex system of deciding which herb will suit your purposes, you can make your magical workings more powerful by paying attention to some of these nuances.

Essentially, different scents, herbs, flowers and plants have their own specific vibrations. Their essences should be worn on your skin (you can make up your own combinations using essential oils or flower waters), burned in an oil burner, inhaled from a cloth, diffused in a bath or bowl of steam, or burned as incense sticks. Many plants, herbs and spices, however used, contain gentle yet effective energies which will affect not only your wishing ceremonies, but also your moods, associations and emotions, which can assist in carrying your wonderful Self in the direction of your dreams. Lifted up on incense smoke, for example, your wish is carried out to the wider Universe. Try making your own, out of any or all of your power plants, woods, flowers, shrubs, trees or herbs!

Thirty-three magical, mythical plants are: Cocoa, rosemary, tobacco, thyme, wheat, coffee, sugar cane, cinnamon, hemp, tea, pumpkin, foxglove, incense, amanita (a mushroom), tarragon, pepper, rice, belladonna, reed, ginseng, clove, ginger, sage, maize, mistletoe, lily, mandrake, St John's Wort, poppy, peyote, cinchona, verbena and the vine *.

*. How many of your Geminian 'lucky plants' (listed under the next sub-category, 'Your Lucky Plants, Herbs, Spices', etc.) can be found on this Magical 33 List?

YOUR LUCKY PLANTS, HERBS, SPICES, TREES, SHRUBS, FLOWERS, SCENTS, OILS & INCENSE

Horse Chestnut, Vervain, Cannabis, Coca, Forsythia, Maidenhair, Nacissus, Mullein, Caraway, Poppy, Rose, Parsley, Hazel, Elecampane, Azalea, Knotted Figwort, Fern, Bittersweet, Marjoram, Snapdragon, Lavender, Yarrow, Tansy, Yerba Santa, Hyssop, Coltsfoot, Horehound, Lemon Balm, Dill, Meadowsweet, Madder, Woodbine, Dog-grass, Skullcap, Cinquefoil, Lobelia, Flax, Aniseed, Myrtle, Lily of the Valley, and all nut-bearing trees. *

For Mercury ★ Vervain, Lungwort, Sweet Marjoram, Aniseed, Olive. As Mercury relates to the Air element, the plants associated with it often contain divided leaves or stalks. Coriander, Fenugreek, Licrorice Roots are all related to this planet *

* Some plant products can be poisonous, toxic, hallucinogenic or even fatal if consumed. Always research first.

YOUR SPECIAL POWER FLOWERS

GEMINI IN GENERAL ★ Lavender

OTHER BIRTH FLOWERS ★ Iris, Myrtle & Snapdragon

MAY BORN ★ Lily of the Valley ★ Lily of the Valley is a very auspicious birth flower, symbolising joy, optimism, and bright, new beginnings throughout life. Lily of the Valley signals the return of happiness.

JUNE BORN ★ Rose ★ Love is the magnificent birth gift of the popular rose, with most representing aspects of love, affection or feeling - rosebuds signifying unawakened love, red roses deep emotions, white roses purity and innocence, yellow roses joy and friendship, pink roses gentle emotions and gratitude, orange roses passion and desire, and black roses death and farewells. The rose has always symbolised beauty, love and fertility. It was sacred to Aphrodite and Venus, the Greek and Roman goddesses of love. The Romans often planted roses on graves, as they regarded it as a symbol of rebirth. In Islam the rose is associated with paradise, and in the Christian tradition, the rose represents the Virgin Mary's purity and beauty. One ancient Christian legend says that until Adam and Eve were expelled from the Garden of Eden roses had no thorns; God added these to remind people that they no longer lived in a perfect world.

YOUR FOODS

Make it snappy, make it smart, and don't weigh the quicksilver Gemini down. Think of the most sophisticated snack food in the world and then serve with nonchalance. Pulsating to the beat of the restlessness of the Twins is a taste for the fun and offbeat. Any food which can be shared in a social setting, such as potato wedges, fairy bread, nachos, hors d'ouvres, platters, footy franks (Australian for mini hotdogs) - in fact, all quick and easy party-style foods. Fun-loving and experimental, Gemini will try anything once - and then again and again until they become bored and move onto the next latest food fad. You love most cuisines, as all types of foods appeal to you, and the more variety the better, preferably in the one dish.

You often find yourself eating at strange hours or on the run as you flit from one activity to the next, and think nothing of having fast takeaway food every other day for the simple reason that it is *fast*. You are essentially a versatile eater and easy to please, however you don't like dense foods which weigh down your restless spirit or hinder your mobility in any way. If anything, 'mind and brain foods', such as oily fish and most seeds and nuts, suit the Geminian body, spirit and psyche; these will keep your overactive mind on an even keel and your overall health in balance too. Stimulating, exciting, varietal and colourful plates are your style. Overall, the quicker, easier and less fussy a food is, the more appealing you will find it! Slow-cooked and home-style taste good, but you are not patient enough to endure the wait. You can be changeable too, so one week you will crave chocolate, the following Scotch eggs, and the next you will eat boiled lollies for breakfast, lunch and dinner. Presentation matters little to you, as most food goes straight from plate to mouth with no time to savour the visual layouts or artistry of your order. Fast, adventurous, convenient, interesting and spirited are definitely on the menu for the Gemini.

GEMINI POWER FOODS

"Let food be your medicine; let medicine be your food."
Hippocrates

Fragrant, Herby, Green, Gamey, Subtle and Bittersweet characterise Gemini-style foods. Bird Meats such as Chicken, Goose, Duck and Turkey, Hare, Venison, Legume Vegetables (Peas, French Beans, Runner Beans, Lentils, Haricot and Broad Beans), Vegetables Grown Above the Ground, Nuts (Hazelnuts, Almonds, Walnuts, Coconuts), Fennel, Asparagus, Okra, Figs, Sprouts, Mushrooms, Carrots, Non-Cereal Seeds, Mulberries And Pomegranates also appeal to the Gemini palate. Your power beverages are Anything Caffeinated (but don't overdo it!), Champagne, Energy Drinks, Sparkling Drinks, Soda Pops and Alco Pops. *

* Caution: Always use essential oils, alcohol and/or herbs with caution and research each one prior to use, as not all are safe for use by certain people, or under certain conditions such as pregnancy, intoxication or illness. Some

herbs and oils may be hallucinogenic, toxic in high doses, or produce other undesirable effects, and may be considered potentially harmful or hazardous if used or consumed before operating machinery, driving, or combined with alcohol or other drugs. Always consult a qualified practitioner or undertake thorough research from reliable sources before use or consumption of any of the listed essential oils, herbs or foods.

YOUR LUCKY WOODS ★ ELDER, FILBERT & BEECH
(Great to make magic wands out of!)

Native Americans referred to trees as 'Standing People' because they stand firm, obtaining strength from their connection with the Earth. They therefore teach us the importance of being grounded, while at the same time listening to, and reaching towards, our higher aspirations. In Norse mythology, Yggdrasil, the tree of life, is a cosmic map that represents all life. The tree has its roots in the Underworld, is linked to the Earth through its trunk and its branches reach into the air of the Otherworld of spirit. The dryad, or tree's spirit, needs to be respected and asked when 'taking' from a tree for the purposes of magic.

The essence of tree magic lies in understanding the qualities of each type. These can be drawn on for such things as healing and spell-casting. For example, the rowan tree grows high up the sides of mountains, often in hard-to-reach places, so if you need to develop tenacity or access to difficult spiritual spaces, you can call on this tree; the oak tree is durable and strong, so if you are needing fortification or firmness, you can gain power from this tree. When respected as living, breathing beings, trees can provide insights into the workings of Nature, cycles, and our own inner essence. Each birth time is associated with a particular kind of tree, the basic qualities of which complement the nature of those born during that time. Appreciate the beauty of your affinity tree and study its nature carefully, for it has a connection with your own nature and lessons to impart.

ELDER ★ The elder is considered a magical and holy tree by various cultures of western and northern Europe. Truly ancient, vestiges of its existence have been found at Stone Age sites. It was believed that elder could not be struck by lightning, and so was planted nearby houses for protection. If struck down, the resilient elder can grow from the smallest stump, and on battlefields it is among the first of the trees to spring back and return life to the destroyed land. The stems of the elder branches, their pith removed, were worn as magical amulets to protect the wearer from harm and also to bring health and good luck to the wearer.

Elder carries properties of exorcism, healing, purification and protection. Elderberries, blossoms or leaves hung over doorways of houses, are said to drive away spirits, serpents and burglars. One old magical chant hails elder as a bringer of prosperity: "Elder over the doorway, fortune over the threshold." But it can be used by the druids, or tree spirits, for both good *and* bad magic. As a sacred tree of the Celtic calendar, it can be used to bless and heal, but as ruler of the thirteenth tree month, the elder also has unlucky associations and, in the past, would have been used in dark magic to curse.

In Irish folklore, it is said that the sidhe- or elf-arrows were fashioned of elder and that the most potent witches' wand was one formed from an elder bough. Considered the tree of transformation, elder is the guardian of the thirteenth month of the Celtic tree calendar. This 'month' is three days long and contains both the end of the year (Halloween) and the beginning of the New Year (All Soul's Day). Celtic tree lore regards the elder as the tree of regeneration, representing 'death in life and life in death'. If it is allowed, this tree can imprint into your consciousness the sensation of harmony which arises from following one's inner prompting and experiencing the new life that rises out of death.

Elder types tend to be wild, free spirits. However, you may be misjudged as an outsider due to your tendency to be withdrawn in spite of your outwardly extroverted nature. Deeply thoughtful and with a philosophical leaning, you genuinely strive to be helpful to others, but your brutal honesty can sometimes trip you up and hinder any assistance offered.

BEECH ★ Beech is traditionally known as 'Queen of the Forest', because this tree is seen as the female counterpart to the oak, the 'King of the Forest'. The words for 'book' and 'beech' are of the same origin due to the historical use of the tree - closely grained and easily smoothed, beech wood was made for writing tablets. Therefore, it is also connected with ancient wisdom.

YOUR SACRED CELTIC CALENDAR TREES
★ HAWTHORN OR OAK

HAWTHORN ★ (13 May - 9 June)
OAK ★ (10 June - 7 July)

The Celts and other ancient peoples had many beliefs and traditions based around the magical lore of trees. The system of Celtic tree astrology was developed out of a natural connection with the Druids' knowledge of Earth cycles and their reverence for the sacred knowledge they believed was held by trees. The Druids had a profound connection with trees and regarded them as vessels of infinite wisdom. Their calendar, being based on a Lunar year of thirteen months, contains a tree for each of these Lunar months, corresponding with (but not exactly) each of the twelve western astrology zodiac signs, which are based on the Solar calendar. Because there are some crossovers, I have included two possible trees for your zodiacal birth period.

HAWTHORN ★ With its white flowers (virginal), red berries (fertility) and sharp thorns (maturity), the hawthorn tree symbolises the three aspects of the Mother Goddess: those of maiden, mother and crone. It is suitable for use by those interested in exploring the Female Mysteries.

Throughout Western Europe, the hawthorn is greatly esteemed as a magical tree bearing protective and visionary powers in addition to its renown amongst herbalists as a heart-healer. The haw in the word means 'hedge', as the thorny-branched trees, which attain a height of up to thirty feet, were planted as hedgerows to separate fields and prevent grazing animals from passing into a neighbour's meadow by virtue of the tree's inch-long thorns. In the European autumn time, the creamy hawthorn blossoms transform into clusters of ruby-red berries and the waxy leaves turn crimson.

Hawthorn has a magical reputation and association with being a portal into 'other worlds'. In Celtic tradition, it was believed that a hawthorn tree found growing with oak and ash was a sacred place in which fairies dwelled, and that if one slept under the hawthorn at Full Moon in May or on May Eve, that one would behold entrance into the land of the sprites. It certainly couldn't hurt to try!

The wood of the hawthorn is fine-grained and therefore suitable for carving delicate items and magical objects. Some traditions even believe hawthorn can carry our wishes into the ether. In times past, travellers hung bits of ribbon on the thorns of this holy tree, murmuring wishes into the cloth. When moved by the wind, these strips whisper the wishes into the ears of fairies who whimsically bestow gifts upon humans. And like many relatives of the rose tree, hawthorn can also be used in love spells to attract one's true love. As the guardian of the doorway to fairy realms, hawthorn wisely discerns the right timing for a wounded heart to open. Hawthorn berries and blossoms can be used to ease the grief of a broken heart and also to open it up to new love.

Hawthorn types are the grand illusionists of the Celtic tree system. You are not what you appear to be. Your outward persona is different to your inner self. While appearing to live a seemingly average life, inside you are burning with the passion of an inexhaustible creative flame. Versatile and well-adjusted, you can adapt to most life situations easily. With a healthy sense of humour and a clear understanding of irony, you are naturally curious and have a broad interest in a wide variety of topics. Possessing amazing insights and the ability to see the bigger picture, you often under-credit yourself for your astute observations.

OAK ★ Oak wood corresponds to the element of Water and the planets Jupiter and Mars, and is a symbol of strength, sovereignty, courage, wisdom, wealth, honesty, toughness, endurance, rulership, nobility, generosity, justice, protection, bravery and power. With its towering height and wide girth, it also symbolises and bestows luck, vigour, love, potency, health and prosperity. The mighty oak tree has a wide trunk, very deep roots and deeply lobed leaves. The older a tree, the larger it will be and mature trees can be well over 1,000 years old (their life span is up to 2,000 years). Held sacred in ancient times, its noble attributes have long been harnessed for use in magic, and today the oak is still valued for its great strength and durability.

Oak is known as the 'King of Trees' and has a strong association with English woodlands, which has its origins in Britain's Pagan past. It is connected with the Summer Solstice, its wood being used to fuel the sacred Midsummer fires. It also has links with royalty and kingship: King Arthur's round table was fabled to have been created from a single cross section of a large oak. In the 'old days', front doors were usually made from oak; this was because, although the thickness of the wood helped to keep the warmth in and unsavoury guests out, its magical properties also provided strength, fertility and protection to the house or building. The word 'druid' originates from the Celtic word 'duir', meaning 'oak' or 'door'. It was believed that the oak was a portal to the spirit world and nature gods were worshipped in oak tree groves.

Acorn nuts, the Divine fruit of the mighty oak, are said to increase fertility, sexual potency, longevity, 'immortality' and youthfulness, fostering virility partly through the sensuality of their creamy texture and smoky flavour, as well as the protein richness they offer. Both nut and cone have been used magically in fertility charms. Acorns are also omens of wealth, happiness and extremely good fortune. The acorn and the tree from which it comes, is a portent which signifies successful outcomes to any venture you want to undertake, and prosperity and growth in the future.

Furthermore, the oak tree's essence helps boost energy levels and to achieve our goals and manifest our desires. Oak is a grounding wood, offering the gifts of stability and strength; imbued with the tree's powerful properties, it can be used to make magical tools or charms. The power and durability of the oak tree are demonstrated by the fact its root system extends as far beneath the Earth as its branches stretch above it. Its strength is further symbolised by enduring what others around it cannot; it remains strong through challenges, and is regarded as being almost immortal, as is often attested by its long life and ability to survive fire, lightning strikes and other similar devastations. Oak is one of the most sacred trees, traditionally prized by the Celts and Druids, the tree's commanding presence signifying true alignment of purpose, balance and fortitude, and Witches often danced beneath the oak tree during ritual. Carrying any part of the oak tree draws good luck to you, but remember first to ask for permission and above all, to show recognition and gratitude for this wood's amazing gifts.

Oak types are the great stabilisers and protectors of the Celtic tree system. You are gifted with a strong, nurturing, generous and helpful spirit, and a voice for the underdog. You are the 'gentle giant' crusader who exudes an easy confidence and naturally assumes everything will always work out well. Having a deep respect for history and ancestry, you love to impart your knowledge of the past to others. You need structure and control over your life, and a large family setting suits you best, ensuring a long, happy and full life.

ESPECIALLY FOR AUSTRALIANS
(OF ALL ZODIAC SIGNS)

If you live in Australia, here are two Australian-based magical woods, for those who prefer to source their woods closer to home and nature. Australia has a less documented history than many European civilisations, but still has no less mythology and legends swirling in its mists of time.

EUCALYPTUS ★ Eucalyptus is very plentiful and has a wonderfully intoxicating, distinctive, clean aroma which is reminiscent of the continent's vast areas of bushland, and has played an important ceremonial and medicinal role in the culture of Australian Aborigines, who have inhabited the nation for 40,000 to 50,000 years. Eucalyptus is a wood of feminine energy whose elemental association is Earth and main origin is Australia. One of the strongest healing woods known, eucalyptus wood has been used for centuries for medicinal as well as ritualistic purposes. Heady and Earthy, the energy of this wood is clean and pure. Eucalyptus is recommended for the promotion of good, robust health, and is also related to luck, especially if regarding knowledge. An excellent tool in divination, particularly when worn as a charm to invoke luck, it brings the wearer or user good fortune when used in rituals seeking positive results.

LEOPARDWOOD (or LACEWOOD) ★
Leopardwood or the Leopard Tree, so named because of its spotted wood, carries the energies of both the masculine and the feminine, Mars (Aries, Scorpio) and Venus (Taurus, Libra), and its main affinity is with the Water element (Cancer, Scorpio, Pisces). Leopardwood is a very useful tool for divination and is associated with positive luck, earning it the label 'gambler's wood'. Overall, its energy is very positive, making it an ideal wood for use in almost any ritual or spell, especially those concerning luck, magic and divination.

THE POWER OF LOVE

Each Sun sign exudes their own love and romance style. This style is an energy unique to that sign, and has the power to magnetise to that person their true, soulful match. Unhappy or unsuccessful relationships are often the result of incompatible Sun signs, personal values, goals, hopes, viewpoints or expectations. I believe everyone has a perfect soul partner (or three!) who is especially for them, and just knowing that special person or persons are out there can illuminate your life's romantic path. In this lifetime, we may not find that person or persons, but can still experience the joys and wonders of many other significant relationships which enrich and add tremendous meaning to our lives. Some partnerships are only fleeting, but the feelings they give us can last a lifetime, while others are more enduring, and the rewards they give us and lessons they teach us can last a lifetime too. Small gestures of love on a frequent basis, consistent nurturing and communication, and making the effort to understand each other, are just four ways to keep the Fires of passion and romance burning long after the initially roaring Fire has diminished into glowing embers.

Your whole natal chart would need to be examined to form an overall picture of your romantic nature, and although the Sun is a fantastic starting point, it is not the sole consideration. Regarding these other planets, in Carl Jung's studies on psychological astrology, and in traditional synastry (the comparing of two people's natal charts to determine overall compatibility), the harmonious link between the Sun in one person's chart and the Moon in the other's (usually the man's Sun and the woman's Moon) is considered the best indication for a happy and enduring relationship. More specifically, the sextile aspect, an angle of 60 degrees, appeared most frequently between the Sun of one and the Moon of the other in fulfilling relationships. Other positive planetary contacts, such as one person's Moon to another's Venus, or the Mars to the Moon (again, traditional indications of attraction and harmony) also occurred frequently.

The feminine personal planets in a male's chart (Moon and Venus), and the masculine personal planets in a female's chart (Sun and Mars) tell a lot about the inner self and how this is projected onto relationships. However helpful chart analysis is in telling a story about your relationship style and approach, it all depends not on your chart, but on what you do with the resources at your disposal, which your chart can indeed tell you a lot about. Relationships and marriages involving harmonious planetary and zodiacal energies between the two people tend to last longer because they are simply more 'flowing' and easier.

The signs in which the four personal and 'relationship' planets - the Sun, the Moon, Venus and Mars - are placed, coupled with the aspects they make with the other planets in the chart, give important clues into understanding the often unconscious drives within you that shape your relating style, tastes, mannerisms and patterns.

Expanding upon the other planetary considerations is beyond the scope of this book, but it is useful to know, particularly if you are interested in examining the dynamics of a current relationship a bit deeper, or are wishing to attract a new one into your life. But for now, your Sun sign is a wonderful place to start! Your Solar sign is regarded as being at the core of the complex - and very fun - study of relationships! So for now, we will begin this study of love with your essence, your core self, the brightest light shining from within - your Sun sign!

SOME LUCKY-IN-LOVE TIPS
GENERAL HINTS

★ To attract and retain love, the Heart chakra (an energy centre within the body) needs to be balanced and clear from blockages. The Heart chakra is located in the region of the physical heart. Its Sanskrit name is *anahata*, and its symbol is a twelve-petal green lotus flower whose centre contains a green circle and two intersecting triangles making up a six-pointed star representing balance (and also could be said to symbolise six as the number of Venus). Its element is Air and its colour is green. Balance in this chakra is expressed as unconditional love for ourselves and others. Crystals that can be used to cleanse and balance this chakra are mostly green and pink stones.

★ Pink candles (two, representing a couple, or six, representing Venus, is preferable) can be used in love spells.

★ Any 'love-attracting' wishing rituals should be done on a Friday (ruled by Venus) night around the time of the New Moon (signifying the principle of increase and growth).

★ Basil, otherwise known as witch's herb or St Joseph's wort, is said to be the most potent lover herb of all. Basil vibrates to the energy of Mars, which is all about lust and sexual energy, and it is used prolifically in all sorts of love potions and rituals throughout the world.

★ Ginger has a reputation as a potent sexual tonic and aphrodisiac *. Arousing and warm, it can increase sensual vitality, particularly in men. Being warming and spicy, its vibration aligns with Mars. Saffron is also regarded as a potent, albeit expensive, aphrodisiac!

★ Wear red and pink (associated with Mars and Venus respectively), as these colours in all their shades are said to incite passion, lust and romance. Green is also connected with the heart by virtue of its association with the Heart chakra and the planet Venus, and its links with fertility, nature, abundance of all kinds, and new growth.

★ Call upon some higher spiritual help. When working your 'love magic', some planetary influences, goddesses and gods that you can call upon are: Aphrodite, Venus and Eros/Cupid, and other lesser known deities such as Juno Lucina, Demeter, Freya, Ishtar, Circe and Hathor.

★ The planet Venus has developed a rich culture of gods and goddesses associated with her varying levels of love and passion. These include the virgin - Brighid; the fertile woman - Aphrodite, (the Greek goddess); and of course Venus (the Roman equivalent); the mother and provider - Demeter; and desirous or physical love - Eros/Cupid (Venus's son).

★ The pine tree is sacred to Adonis (Venus's lover) and is said to balance the male and female energies. Pine is cleansing and protective and, as an evergreen, symbolises life. Its cones represent fertility.

★ Cardamom is said to have aphrodisiac qualities

★ The three almost universally recognised symbols of love are the goddesses Venus and Aphrodite, and the Cupid. Venus is the patroness of flowers and vegetation, and represents the regenerative cycle of creation, as well as beauty, herbs and physical love. She can be called upon for general love wishes and rituals. The dove, roses, rings, copper, apples, rosemary and the ankh are some of her sacred symbols. Aphrodite is a Greek goddess who has the ability to bring lovers together. Her names means 'of the sea' as she is believed to have been born of the foam of the ocean. She can be called upon in ceremonies and spells for affection, love, marriage and partnership. Some of her associated symbols are the Flower of Aphrodite, swans, dolphins, frankincense and myrrh. Cupid, the cherubic winged boy with a bow and arrow, is the Roman name, and

Eros is the Greek name for the same deity. The son of Venus/Aphrodite, he is an aspect that represents lustful love and desire.

★ Heartsease, another name for the wild pansy, Latin viola tricolour, was one of the most popular additives to the love potions of the ancient Romans and Greeks.

★ In centuries past, when people were more in tune with nature and its cycles, ceremonies, rituals and festivals were held on certain dates or times of year. The following are some examples, and you can reawaken their powers through craft and ceremony: February 2 is Bridhid's Day, or Bride's Day, and represents the white goddess; February 14 is Valentine's Day, traditionally the greatest and most well-known love 'celebration' of the year; March 1 is one of the festival days of Juno Lucina, the light bearer and goddess of women and marriage; the month of April is especially linked to the love goddess Aphrodite; the Summer solstice which falls on or around June 21 is an important time for reconnecting with the spirit of love, fertility and marriage; August 1 is the first of three harvest festivals in the Celtic calendar: The Harvest Festival honours Demeter, the goddess of love, as bountiful mother and faithful wife; the Festival of Lights, Diwali, in October, is sacred to Lakshmi, the Hindu goddess of happiness, love, and good fortune; the Winter solstice which falls on or around December 21, marks the turning point from long dark nights to lengthening days, and is the time of the wheel of love when virgin goddesses gave birth to their children - it is also fittingly symbolised by evergreens such as pine, ivy and holly; in Mexico, December 31, the last night of the year, is traditionally 'wishing night' and is an opportune time to make a wish for a lover in the coming year, using evergreen branches to enhance your request.

* The term 'aphrodisiac' is derived from Aphrodite, the Greek goddess of love, beauty, lust and sensuality

★ GEMSTONES ★

When it comes to calling love into your life using crystals, the general rule is that any of the pink or green stones are closely aligned with matters of the heart and can therefore help you to entice the affections you seek. Although your Sun sign has its very own special gemstones, outlined elsewhere in the book, the following stones can be used by all the signs (except for the first point, which are your own sign's feature stones), as their energies and qualities contain the power to attract and create love in all its forms, from self-love to deeper soulful connections with another, or to increase states of being which open the heart, thus enhancing your abilities to magnetise love.

★ Alexandrite, Agate and Citrine ★ Using your Geminian luckiest crystals is a fabulous start to working on heightening your romantic zest, and making your sensual energy more potent. Emerald,

Tourmaline, Chrysoprase, Pearl and Moonstone are also useful in raising your attracting powers.

★ Rose Quartz is the ultimate love stone. It invites love into your life by helping to open your heart to receive love, and gently reminding you that you are worthy of love. Connected with the Heart chakra, it is the stone of unconditional love, enhancing all forms of it and opening up the heart. It is excellent for increasing self-worth and acceptance. The colour of rose quartz is pink, the colour of Venus, the amorous planet of desire and nurturance. Balancing and calming, it helps to heal emotional pain. Wear this stone, keep some beside your bed, or sleep with some under your pillow to remind you that love it coming your way - and that you whole*heart*edly deserve it!

★ Green Aventurine is considered the 'opportunity and luck stone'. Connected with the Heart chakra, it helps us to recognise opportunities and is said to place us exactly where we need to be for good things to transpire, as energetically it opens our mind and heart to increased perception to recognise lucky elements. It also promotes new growth, optimism, and is an overall attractor of good fortune, adventure and abundance.

★ Jade, on a spiritual level, has an affinity with the Heart chakra. It harmonises relationships, and encourages compassion and the establishment of strong bonds.

★ Emerald is reputedly a stone of constancy in love, and is said to have been brought to Earth from the planet Venus. Because it is green, it also holds deep associations with the Heart chakra.

★ Rhodochrosite can be used to attract one's soul mate. This stone, as with all the pink stones, can be used as an effective love magnet. It encourages you to appreciate yourself by teaching you that you are worthy of love, wholeness and happiness - and so opening you up to receive.

★ Malachite, Citrine, Rhodonite, Moonstone, Morganite, Beryl, Ruby, Mangano Calcite, Garnet, Red and Pink Tourmaline, Tugtupite, Rutilated Quartz, Lodestone, Peridot and Lapis Lazuli are also known for their love properties, and can be used or worn to invite romance into your life, or to bring and retain enduring love.

★ Clear Quartz can be used with any of these listed crystals to amplify their metaphysical properties.

★ Shells: Although shells are not technically a crystal, but rather a natural elemental material, they are associated with love and are sacred to Aphrodite, the Greek love goddess, and are often used in magic talismans to attract romance.

★ ESSENTIAL OILS ★

The following essential oils are known for their aphrodisiac or love-attracting properties also, and can be worn as perfumes on the skin, used in an oil burner or vaporiser, dispersed in a bath, used in spell-casting and wishing rituals, sprinkled on your pillow to imbue your dreams with inspired romantic notions, or in any other creative ways you can think of! **

★ Essential oils, flowers and herbs which contain natural pheromones or like substances, or increase pheromone levels in the body, are: Lavender, Frankincense, Jasmine, Nutmeg, Ylang Ylang, Sandalwood, Patchouli and Asian Agarwood (Oud).

★ The prime love oil, which holds universal appeal, is rose. Reputedly excellent for both the mind and body, roses are the basis of more than 95 per cent of women's fragrances, and the petals have a long tradition of uplifting the spirits and soothing the soul. *Rosa damascena* is believed to be good for attracting love, while *R. centifolia*, the French rose oil base, is regarded as an aphrodisiac. Rose is traditionally accepted as the all-encompassing universal fragrance of love, blessed with a reputation for opening up the hearts of all those who come under its spell.

★ Cedarwood oil has been used since ancient times in incense and perfumes. Its deep, woody scent helps to stimulate the Base chakra, increasing sexual passion and desire. Its sedative qualities aid relaxation and encourage openness. In herbal magic, it is also associated with spells for wealth and abundance.

★ Neroli, Geranium, Almond (as a base), Basil, Thyme, Vetiver, Gardenia, Vanilla, Rose Otto, Apple, Cardamom, Lotus, Orange, Ginger, Bergamot, Rosewood and Clary Sage are also exquisitely seductive and sensual, and can be used in any way you like to bring to you that which your heart desires. These oils, when mixed with your own pheromones and magical intentions, will naturally enhance your point of attraction!

** Always research first and use with caution.

GEMINI ★ LOVE STYLE

"He's truly the Mercurius of alchemy, the translator and the transformer, for he can show with the magic wand of his wit the distant mountain heights where the air is clear."
***Star Signs For Lovers*, Liz Greene, Arrow Books, 1980**

"It's true that when you're in love with a Gemini you won't walk alone. You most certainly won't. You'll have at least two people to walk with you - and both of them will be him. He was born under the sign of the Twins, you know. In his case, they're never identical Twins … (for) the dual nature of Gemini combines two completely different personalities."
Linda Goodman

To the Twins, love is one big magical carpet ride through a sparkling, star-spangled galaxy, either a daring adventure … or nothing at all. Hot and cold, up and down, over and out - your fickle nature in romantic endeavours can drive your lovers crazy! Life without romantic fun, magical unions and grand scale love affairs is like champagne without bubbles to you, and being such a flirt who loves to bedazzle, outwit and impress others, you rarely fail to attract many and varied experiences of the heart. Your ideal partner is likely to be younger and the match based on affection and companionship and a 'meeting of the minds' rather than deep, sentimental romantic love. You are one Air sign that really prefers friendship to love; your chosen partner should always be your friend too. To you, emotions are mushy and rather illogical, yet you often have an uncanny and inexplicable way of attracting feeling types, who both fascinate and terrify you at the same time. Emotional or not, if your partner can understand that Gemini is the eternal butterfly and allows for freedom of mobility accordingly, you will derive a sense of satisfaction from your partnership. But often you will infuriate your lovers by not extending the same consideration and being impossible to pin down; however, you will always win them back over by playing the youthful, fun-loving clown. Gemini is never quite ready to become too deeply involved. Seeing so many choices, you hesitate to commit yourself, for by fixing yourself on one thing, you're afraid you might miss something better, which is why your emotional exchanges so often only skim the top, even when you are a fully-fledged grown-up. Romance to you is one big, amusing game, and your restlessness means that it can be hard for you to sit still, let alone commit the rest of your life to the one person. Once and if you do marry, however, you have the potential to make a committed, if a little inconsistent husband or wife, but your flirty nature never quite takes flight.

Watching your wandering ways could prove helpful too, as you may unwittingly drive your partner away by charming and socialising your way through every party and event going, and by being too busy with too many things to spend the necessary quality time with your beloved. You are incredibly open and friendly, but you may also come across as insincere and scatter your energies too far for them to be effective. As a lover and in relationships, you are afraid of deep emotional involvement and may find it difficult to sustain close relationships, because this may mean toning down your lifestyle to accommodate the needs of another, but you can become your partner's best friend forever once committed. Perhaps Linda Goodman summed it up best when she stated, "Loving a Gemini is easy and fun, if you don't try to get too close. There's an inner core that belongs only to him that he'll never share with another human being, even you. Keep things cool and light, and don't be overly passionate or dramatic." After all, for the Twins, love is fast, breezy, edgy, flirty and above all, *fun*!

LUCKY IN LOVE? GEMINI ★ COMPATIBILITY

* Please note the following is based on your Sun sign alone. For a whole and integrated approach to relationship compatibility, your whole natal chart would need to be taken into consideration. Synastry (*syn*: acting or considered together, united; *astry*: pertaining to the stars) is a branch of astrology which delves into more complex areas, and is based upon the natal charts of the two people concerned, to determine overall compatibility, potential conflicts and suitability based upon celestial influences. For the purposes of length, the below information is simplified and only refers to Sun sign connections.

Gemini ★ Aries ♊ ♈

Cheekiness, childishness and mischief reign supreme with this combination. The Ram and the Twins make a stimulating mix, and you will both talk and laugh non-stop. Ariens and Geminis are both cheerful, lively and entertaining characters. You have much in common, and this is a good combination. The depth and intensity of Arien passion may take you by surprise. Your easygoing, light-hearted ways and Aries's childlike enthusiasm spark a natural friendship and rapport. You even know how to handle the Martian's notorious temper, by making them laugh. Gemini will never hamper Aries's independence or initiative, and Aries is likely to feel inspired by Gemini's lively and friendly company. If used constructively, this is a wonderful match which will fulfil, uplift and inspire both signs. Fire and Air is an agreeable combination, and since you both generate a playful, busy atmosphere, your life together will never have a dull moment. However, the Twins are cunning, cheeky and manipulative, and the uncomplicated Arien spirit may feel irritated or perplexed by Gemini's tricky and changeable nature. But Gemini's wits will usually be a good match for the Aries's fighting spirit and dynamism, and for the most part you will find it an easy, enjoyable ride. You both enjoy variety, discovery, exploring, novelty and socialising, but Aries may find Gemini talks a bit much - Aries prefers to act on impulse and ask questions later. One thing is certain with you two: you will both give each other the space you need in the relationship. Gemini is stimulated by Aries's bold, impetuous and amusing behaviours, while Aries is bemused by Gemini's fickle, inconsistent but lovable nature and social charm. Both are inspired and childlike, and will entertain each other for hours with cartwheel competitions, pulling faces and playful affections. Neither of you will take the relationship too seriously, as you know that the most important basis for any successful relationship lies in having fun together, and sharing in the delights of light-hearted friendship.

Overall compatibility rating ★ 8.5 out of 10
Lucky Romance Tip ★ To attract an Aries, wear the colours red or orange, and use the crystal diamond

Gemini ★ Taurus ♊ ♉

The talkative Twins may make the Bull's head spin. It's often one step forward, two steps back, as the Bull closes in and Gemini wriggles free. Taurus is the earthiest sign of all, while Airy Gemini is extremely restless, changeable and fickle - traits which are completely foreign to the immovable Bull. The Twins' love of constant change and variety can be unnerving for Taurus, who likes to stay put and works best in the confines of a consistent routine. Taureans take commitment very seriously, therefore Gemini needs to control his flirtatious behaviour. If you can both overcome your considerable differences, this is potentially a very happy pairing. The earthbound Bull can indeed complement Gemini's flighty fast-paced haste. Even though the Twins find it difficult to tolerate the Bull's possessiveness, the Taurean slow and smooth sensuality may fascinate and intrigue Gemini. The Gemini's Mutable, flexible nature may prove too difficult to handle for the Bull's fixed, steady, consistent nature, and the Gemini fickleness may upset the normally peaceful Taurus's harmony. Gemini may resent being 'possessed' by the security-seeking Bull, and will at all opportunities break free from any restrictions placed upon him - sometimes forever. The Twins are quick-witted and lightning fast with their thoughts, while Taurus likes to mull things over before reaching a very well-considered conclusion; as well, Gemini loves to share, exchange and talk, while Taurus prefers peace, harmony and to keep her ideas to her quiet self. Further, Taurus does not like to analyse or over-think, preferring to live for the sensations of the moment, and this may frustrate the intellectual, ever-thinking Gemini, whose mind sparks in all directions simultaneously. In this partnership, there will be little mental rapport, and although Gemini may be initially attracted to Taurus's deep sensuality and grace of movement, his mind changes like the wind and he may well be off to seek greener pastures as soon as the Bull utters the words 'exclusive relationship'. The Taurus will ultimately perceive the Twins as too spirited and over-the-top, but if she can overcome her over-emphasis on stability, the Gemini can bring the gifts of exuberance, youthful vigour and excitement into their ordinary everyday life, and snuff out any stale boredom for good.

Overall compatibility rating ★ 6 out of 10
Lucky Romance Tip ★ To attract a Taurus, wear the colours pink or green, and use the crystal rose quartz

Gemini ★ Gemini ♊ ♊

Both thinking and mentally-oriented Air signs, ruled by the same planet Mercury, you two have the potential to make beautiful music together. Another Gemini will give you all the space you need in the relationship, and this double dose of such a highly strung, restless sign ensures that life will never be dull or dreary. However, depending on other factors in the birth charts, this pairing can either be excitable, lively, scatterbrained, gossipy, full of change and intellectually stimulating, or full of chaos, confusion and nervous tension. You both enjoy discussion and debate, and there will be plenty to talk about when two chatty Geminians get together. You are both very flirtatious, and serious commitment will need effort. Two Twins up to tricks is even more head-spinning than one. This is a rare, sparkling gem of a romance, where you will both delight in keeping the other guessing. Neither is likely to smother the other, but you may be so busy dashing around and mingling in your many separate activities and friendship circles that you forget to make time for each other! Also, being such a dynamic and charged combination, you may need to consider if there is enough room for four of you in the relationship.

Overall compatibility rating ★ 8.5 out of 10
Lucky Romance Tip ★ To attract a Gemini, wear the colours light blue or yellow, and use the crystal citrine

Gemini ★ Cancer ♊ ♋

Cancer's sentimentality and over-emotionality may make Gemini feel uneasy and may not evoke a deep response in him, as Gemini has little time for fathoming the Crab's deep feelings and incessant moodiness. Overall, these two have very different aims. Gemini loves to talk, but will not necessarily have the sensitivity to Cancer's feelings to say the right things, making it hard to build up trust. The Twins are so busy doing things, that the Crab may often feel neglected. Any sulking that ensues will not be tolerated by the freedom-seeking, mentally-oriented Twins. Gemini wants excitement, while Cancer craves domestic security. If Gemini can curb his restless streak, the Cancerian may trust him with her tender heart and happiness. Cancer's slushy emotions can seem self-indulgent and even petty to Gemini, yet this nurturing Water sign can be just what the Twins need to settle their highly strung nerves. The Crab may prove too emotional and clingy for the footloose and fancy-free Twins, and Cancer will find Gemini's pressing need to be a social butterfly dizzying, and perhaps even hurtful to their highly sensitive nature. Cancer is private while Gemini shares with everyone; Watery Cancer is emotional while Airy Gemini is intellectual; Cancer is home-loving while Gemini feels stifled when domestically 'caged in'; Cancer seeks sentimental love and a meeting of the hearts, while Gemini seeks friendship and a meeting of the minds. Gemini's fickle and changeable nature may unsettle the soft-hearted Cancerian, whose protective, security-seeking nature means her interests lie primarily in home, hearth, children and family.

Overall compatibility rating ★ 5 out of 10
Lucky Romance Tip ★ To attract a Cancerian, wear the colours silver or white, and use the crystal moonstone

Gemini ★ Leo ♊ ♌

You both love to play and joke, so you can have some great fun together. But although Leo is stimulated and intrigued by the tricky, cunning Gemini's cheekiness, he doesn't quite trust it. Leo represents dignity, while Gemini is imprudent. The Twins may find Leo too pompous, and the Lion may see the Twins as frivolous. If you can overcome this mutual disapproval, you may have a stimulating, enlightening relationship. Overall, Fire and Air are a compatible combination. Gemini fans Leo's flames with his wit and charm, but the Lion's delicate pride will be hurt and he will stride away if the Gemini flirts with other people. As Air and Fire blend well together, a healthy, fun-loving rapport can be easily built up between you, which is always a good starting point and foundation for any relationship.

Leo's broad vision and warm nature will appeal to Gemini, but the Lion's desire to be boss and take control of the relationship can sometimes unsettle Gemini's free spirit. These qualities can be used constructively to form a wonderful bond between you, but there will inevitably be clashes of wills, especially if the Gemini takes flight, as he is prone to do on a frequent basis, and the Lion doesn't get his way. Leo needs adoration, praise and to be the centre of attention, and will not always appreciate Gemini's need for sharing and social stimulation with so many others. Leo's pride can be easily wounded by Gemini's independence and lack of consistent affection. Overall, if used positively, the Lion and the Twins can share a joyful and stimulating relationship, if they can overcome their differences. Indeed, Air will usually fuel the Fire here, making it burn bigger and brighter. And if each partner is happy to allow the other to do his/her own thing, this has the potential to be a sparkling union of dazzling proportions.

Overall compatibility rating ★ 8 out of 10
Lucky Romance Tip ★ To attract a Leo, wear the colours gold or orange, and use the crystal ruby

Gemini ★ Virgo ♊ ♍

The trickster Twins are a little flighty for Virgo's more steady, deliberate nature. Yet Gemini's entertaining and stimulating intellect will lift Virgo's Earthy spirits and keep her guessing, which will continue to intrigue the Virgin. Both ruled by Mercury, the planet of intellect and communication, you will have plenty to discuss and a substantial rapport. Yet Virgo's fussy perfectionism can make the Gemini take flight. Earthy Virgo may not approve of this flightiness, but you are potentially a strong couple and a compelling combination. Overall though, Air and Earth generally don't blend well together, and although you share the ruling planet Mercury, this only emphasises a mental and intellectual affinity between your two very different signs, rather than a deep emotional bond. Virgo's nit-picking and fastidiousness will get on Gemini's nerves, and Gemini's fickle and carefree nature will unsettle the orderly, rational and sensible Virgo. The Twins' dispassionate and restless character may resonate with the Virgin's naturally cool and essentially unemotional psyche, but Virgo's natural tendency to anxiety and worrying will irk the much more light-hearted Gemini. Moreover, the Virgin is straight-laced, systematic and pure, while the Twins have an agenda - they are the cunning, manipulative pranksters of the zodiac, which doesn't sit well with the virtuous do-gooder Virgo. Overall, Virgo's pedantic need for logic, detailed analysis and order are the farthest things from the erratic Gemini's mind, and Virgo's meticulous attitudes towards cleanliness and tidiness are not concerns at all for the scatterbrained devil-may-care Gemini. At the end of the romance, the only thing you may find you had in common was your ruling planet, which can very well act as a stimulating catalyst but is just as likely to fizzle out long before it reaches the end of the wire.

Overall compatibility rating ★ 5.5 out of 10
Lucky Romance Tip ★ To attract a Virgo, wear the colours white or yellow, and use the crystal sapphire

Gemini ★ Libra ♊ ♎

Two Air signs tango very nicely, yet Gemini remains an enigma to the Scales. Libra admires the Twins' mental agility yet may find him a little exhausting. Geminian liveliness will boost Libran energy levels, and the placid Libran influence will undoubtedly calm the Twins' restlessness. However, Gemini may not be able to provide the security that Libra is seeking. Two Air signs, both oozing natural charm, make for a fine friendship, but if Gemini would like to be more than friends with the Scales, he will need to curb his talking and listen more. Air harmonises with Air, and these two have the potential to have a delightful and stimulating meeting of the minds. This combination also blends Mercury, the planet of the mind, with Venus, the planet of love, creating a mutual appreciation between you of all that is sociable, beautiful, artistic, refined, interesting and spirited. The two of you together mix intellect, charm and esprit, and you are both flirtatious, so a strong mutual attraction will be likely as soon as you meet. Since these two signs are naturally friendly and need the company of others, they can share these pleasures together. However, Libra's emphasis on close intimate relationships may cause tensions, as Gemini needs to feel free, unencumbered and able to indulge in many adventures and activities. While Gemini talks now and thinks later, Libra uses diplomacy, grace and tact to handle things. Neither will make impossible demands on the other, as both are intellectually-based rather than feeling, smothering types, but this relationship can only work if Libra allows Gemini the freedom to explore and does not demand too much of the Twins. Your intellectual rapport alone however, suggests deep potential here, and can take your relationship to great heights. And one thing is certain, boredom will most certainly never be a feature.

Overall compatibility rating ★ 9 out of 10
Lucky Romance Tip ★ To attract a Libran, wear the colours pink and blue, and use the crystal opal

Gemini ★ Scorpio ♊ ♏

The Twins may seem a bit flippant and superficial for the much deeper and more serious Scorpion. Gemini may also be a bit flighty when the Scorpio is wanting deep discussions. You tend to misunderstand each other. Moreover, Geminians may find it difficult to realise the depth and power of Scorpio emotions. If Gemini's flirtatious ways provoke them to a jealous fury, the Gemini will be taken aback by the heat of the Scorpionic rage. Gemini will certainly feel Scorpio's sting if they try any mental tricks here. Scorpio's moodiness and intensity may make the Twins feel out of their depth, which creates many challenges.

Air and Water don't tend to blend easily, and this is highlighted in this coupling. Scorpio is intensely emotional and naturally possessive, and this doesn't always sit too well with the freedom-loving, flighty and ethereal Gemini. Scorpio may feel rejected and left cold by the Twins' apparent disregard for her complex feelings. If Scorpio tries to dominate or control the impossible-to-pin-down Gemini, the Twins will revolt and promptly skip off to a new venture without looking back. Scorpio is passionate and controlling, while Gemini needs space and freedom to move - both mentally and physically. An attraction between you two is highly likely, as Gemini will be intrigued by the mysterious, brooding Scorpion, and Scorpio in turn will be turned on by the lively, carefree flirt in Gemini. But unless the significant differences in your emotional expression are understood, Scorpio will likely feel that Gemini is too indifferent, inconsistent and restless. Also, Gemini's erratic nature will challenge Scorpio's much more stable, fixed character. If Scorpio seeks to possess and overpower, the Twins will simply wriggle free. Although there are many differences between you, if you can channel your combined forces of intellect and power into a common goal, great achievements are possible in this relationship.

Overall compatibility rating ★ 6.5 out of 10
Lucky Romance Tip ★ To attract a Scorpio, wear the colours red or burgundy, and use the crystal malachite

Gemini ★ Sagittarius ♊ ♐

You and your opposite sign can laugh and chatter together for hours. Both cheeky, witty, lively and curious, Gemini incites the Archer to act on his dreams while Sagittarius respects the Gemini's restless, childish charm. Both Geminians and Sagittarians are footloose novelty-seekers, and in many ways you make a perfect match. Both of you are witty, gregarious and entertaining, and will share a lively and carefree existence. Opposite signs have a lot to teach each other and you both share a love of learning; however different your approaches are. You respect each other's opinions, yet Sagittarius can seem a bit vague and idealistic to the Gemini's more astute way of thinking. Air and Fire have a strong affinity, as do your ruling planets, Mercury and Jupiter. You will probably have a wonderful chemistry between you and make a strong impact on each other, but when the need arises, you both give each other the freedom you so desire. Both being independent and intellectual rather than deeply feeling, you share a need for adventure and busyness, and Gemini is self-sufficient enough to allow the Archer his much-needed independence. Stimulating conversation will not be lacking and you both love to share your sparkling ideas and mingling socially. The Archer has an uncanny ability to bring out the passionate side of the Twins, and Sagittarius's warm wit and charm will win the Gemini over in no time. You are both naturally friendly and gregarious, so are likely to attract and enjoy many resulting social pleasures and events together. If Gemini's superficiality doesn't clash with Sagittarius's broad-minded, far-sighted visions, you have the potential to stretch well into the future together.

Overall compatibility rating ★ 9 out of 10
Lucky Romance Tip ★ To attract a Sagittarius, wear the colour deep purple or royal blue, and use the crystal zircon

Gemini ★ Capricorn ♊ ♑

Gemini bemuses Capricorn with his flighty and childlike wonder and innocence. But the Goat's initial attraction to the Twins may turn to apprehension and withdrawal when she uncovers Gemini's cheeky and nonchalant carelessness, which doesn't sit well with Capricorn's practical, realistic approach to life.

Gemini will appreciate the dry Capricornian sense of humour. However, the Goat tends to take life too seriously, and the Twins may be too flighty for them in turn, although Capricorn can provide Gemini with a much-needed stabilising influence. In return, the Gemini could help Capricorn see the fun side to life.

Overall though, Gemini has very little in common with the Goat. Although he can respect her solid achievements, he may find her wall of staunch reserve and reticence rather off-putting. While Gemini, an Air sign, is changeable, restless, lively, scatterbrained, edgy, stimulating and wayward, Capricorn, an Earth sign, is traditional, sensible, controlled, pragmatic, conventional and structured. Capricorn is tight, sometimes mean and ruthless, and tenacious in her striving for lofty goals and ambitions, while Gemini is carefree but ever-friendly, and independent, determined to reach his many ideals using charm, eloquence, cunning and flying by the seat of his cheeky pants to get where and what he wants.

Indeed, mischievous Geminian behaviour often undermines Capricorn's desire for stability, security and consistency. While the Goat is rigid, cautious, methodical and respectful, the Gemini flits from person to person and adapts to any new situation. However, you do share minds of a high order, and if you can channel your energies into your intellectual rapport and natural respect for each other, a mutually fulfilling relationship could very well unfold. And although your characters are very different, you can enrich each other with your unique gifts. Indeed, the young at heart spirit of the Twins can complement the wisdom and experience of the Goat, providing you are both willing to communicate to find common ground. Your life together may prove challenging at times, because Gemini so often changes direction, whereas steady Capricorn will pursue a goal to its conclusion. Gemini is easily distracted, while

Capricorn has a single-minded vision and stays on the path. In this way, Capricorn rarely understands the highly strung, quicksilver ways of the crafty Twins. However, on the whole, there is something lacking emotionally which can make romance between you difficult and strained.

Overall compatibility rating ★ 6 out of 10
Lucky Romance Tip ★ To attract a Capricorn, wear the colours brown or black, and use the crystal garnet

Gemini ★ Aquarius ♊ ♒

Aquarian eccentricity will amuse and enchant the Twins, and they will be attracted to the sociable side of the Aquarian personality. But Aquarius, being a fixed sign, takes loyalty very seriously, and may not appreciate Gemini's flirtatious bent. You can delight each other with your mental gymnastics and this can be a fine friendship and a sparkling romance. Gemini's easygoing charm will fascinate the more serious Aquarian. Both thinking and mentally-oriented Air signs, you have the potential to make beautiful music together. Gemini can usually accept Aquarius's erratic and detached moods, and both will give each other the space they need in the relationship. Gemini is stimulated by Aquarius's dazzling intellect and Aquarius in turn is inspired by Gemini's lively mind. The headstrong, wilful, stubborn characteristics of the Water Bearer may be trying for the Twins' fickle, Mutable, flexible nature, and Gemini's restlessness may make Aquarius dizzy at times. Similarly, Aquarius's rebelliousness may frazzle and fray the much less complex Twins' nerves. But one thing is certain: The Water Bearer will always keep Gemini on his agile toes and wits! These two can usually work through most differences, however, and there will never be a dull moment, especially in the social arena, in which you both spend most of your time. The unconventional and changeable quality of this relationship helps to keep it interesting, and neither is likely to smother the other, but you both may be so busy mingling in your many separate activities and friendship circles that you forget to make time for each other!

Overall compatibility rating ★ 9 out of 10
Lucky Romance Tip ★ To attract an Aquarian, wear the colours electric blue or turquoise, and use the crystal aquamarine

Gemini ⋆ Pisces ♊ ♓

Pisceans are deeply feeling and idealistic partners, and Gemini's light-hearted and uncomplicated approach to love may upset the Fish. Emotional storms could be triggered by Gemini's flirtatiousness. Pisces, however, will delight in the Twins' playful, romantic gestures. And you both share the changeable and whimsical qualities the Mutable mode endows you with. With Gemini's tendency to play the field and Pisces's vulnerability, it's a small miracle that you two even come together in the first place. This is a challenging duo and the Fish's sensitive nature and changing whims may prove too emotional for

Gemini. But, both being so versatile, you do have the potential to adapt to each other. Gemini can usually accept Pisces's dreamy and elusive nature, but may find it difficult to swallow the Fish's emotions and deep sensitivities. Both will give each other the space they need in the relationship, but for different reasons; Gemini, because he above all seeks freedom of movement, and Pisces because she above all seeks to dream her way through life and live amongst the clouds undisturbed by Earthly concerns.

Gemini is intrigued by Pisces's ethereal and spiritual nature, and Pisces in turn is inspired by Gemini's lively and impressive intellect. However, this is where the similarities and interests in one another may end; the marked contrast between Air and Water is clearly illustrated here. Gemini is logical, factual, mentally-orientated and lives in a thought-based world, whereas Pisces is imaginative, dreamy, feeling, and lives by emotions, impressions and intuition. As a result of these conflicting elemental qualities, Gemini will often be unable to see reason in the illogical ways of Pisces. Both signs are very adaptable and tolerant of other people's ideas, so although you will rarely understand the way the other's mind works, you have the potential of reaching a middle ground and settling in for the ride. Gemini is efficient, active, intellectual, flashy and handy, while Pisces is easily confused, indecisive and for the most part passive. The Fish may spend so long whiling away the hours sitting on the fence, that when she looks around, the Twins have found a new, novel adventure somewhere over the horizon and cannot be seen for the dust they leave behind.

Overall compatibility rating ★ 6 out of 10
Lucky Romance Tip ★ To attract a Pisces, wear the colours mauve or sea green, and use the crystal amethyst

YOUR TAROT CARDS ★ FOR LUCK, MAGIC, ENERGY, ABUNDANCE, QUESTING & MEANING
THE LOVERS, THE MAGICIAN & THE FOOL

Tarot and astrology are inextricably linked. All the cards of the Major Arcana, which comprises 22 of the Tarot's 78 cards, are 'ruled by' or connected with either one of the twelve zodiac signs, the planets and luminaries, or one of the four elements.

The 22 Major Arcana cards contain the richest symbolism of all the cards in the Tarot deck, each carrying a myriad of messages for the reader to decipher. The symbolism contained within these images represents the archetypal aspects of your character. It also describes the path your soul takes through each stage of life, revealing clues through which you can explore different parts of yourself. Each of the cards also represents an aspect of universal human experience and has a name that either directly conveys the meaning of the card, such as Strength or Justice, or depicts individuals that represent these human archetypes, such as the Hermit or the Empress. The illustrations on each card contain one or more figures and tuning into a card's imagery enables you to grasp its meaning intuitively. Consider the demeanour of the characters, whether it is day or night, the background, any symbols, the buildings, the colours, the vegetation, the weather and the season. Every card has its own story to impart, and through entering that story you can gain deeper insights into the full picture of your journey so far, as well as illuminating your path ahead.

I have outlined three cards here for your sign: The Lovers, The Magician and The Fool, all of which have links to your zodiac sign itself Gemini, your ruling planet Mercury, and your element of Air. All three cards will have special meaning for your sign, and can carry powerful messages and lessons for you to reflect upon.

★ THE LOVERS ★
Ruled by Gemini

Keywords ★ Choices, Options, Opposites

★ KEY THEMES ★
★ Choice ★ Desire ★ Decision ★ Temptations ★ Union ★ Reconciliation ★ Harmony ★ Sacrifice ★ Indecision ★ Trials and Options that May be Linked to Relationships ★ Relationship Decisions Resulting in Stability ★ A Return to Good Health ★ Carefully Weighing Options ★ Need for Balance ★ Marriage and Weddings ★ Complementary Opposites

Number ★ 6
Astrological Sign ★ Gemini

THE MESSAGE ★ Traditionally an image of duality and choice, the Lovers represent the yin and yang forces of the Universe and their natural attraction for each other. Love, or the coming together of these complementary forces, can occur on many levels. In its deeper, more esoteric form, the image refers to the merging of these opposite qualities within a being, which leads to wholeness. In Tarot the Lovers usually signifies a sexual union is in process. When the Lovers appears in a reading, it signals that a significant decision or relationship is on your mind; you are either working on a partnership in which you are already involved, or preparing for a liaison with a new partner. It may be intimate or romantic in nature, or it may be a close but platonic friendship.

In any case, being a lover is on your mind. Feeling the pull of this magnetic force, you face a choice. If the question is something to the tune of, "Are we going to be lovers or not?" and you feel passionate excitement about this query, then you can be assured you will soon be taking a journey to a deeper place, but to do so, you are asked to trust, to risk and to face the unknown. The Lovers also indicates a time to make an important decision about your life, for any conclusions you reach now will significantly influence your future, making it all the more important to weigh up your options carefully and thoroughly consider all angles. A decisive point has been reached, and this important choice must be made with reference to true desires rather than duty. A dramatic change of attitudes will indeed lead to happier times.

THE AWAKENING ★ You come to understand that your relationships with others are an outer expression of the desire for inner connection, and that loving another person helps you to discover new aspects of yourself, and so to grow. If you fall passionately in love, it will teach you the difference between co-dependency and genuine caring and sharing. With The Lovers, you learn more about yourself through another. Your relationships reflect your own inner balance. Though this card usually indicates a love affair is or is about to be in progress, the choice is not always romantic or sexual in nature but may be between any two allurements.

SYMBOLISM *★ The young man in the Lovers image holds the woman's hand to make his feelings known. She looks away uncertainly, seemingly contemplating whether or not to accept his offer of love, symbolising the choices this card indicates need to be made. They are watched by an elderly figure, a wise old man, who symbolises the knowledge of lifelong experience. He is armed with this wisdom, well aware of the decisions that lie before the young lovers, even if they are not.

The Cupid is a character from classical mythology, and is pictured in this card peeking out from the clouds, preparing to fire his arrows of love at the woman, as if imploring her to make the right decision, one that is based on sound consideration of all the available facts.

The Lovers can represent both virtue and vice - the basic alternatives. This card obviously refers to strong emotions, and choices of the heart which cannot be made by logic alone. In older decks this card shows a young man who has to make a decision between two women while the abovementioned Cupid hovers above, aiming his arrow. Later versions of the Lovers replaced Cupid with the fiery archangel

St Michael, and the group below by figures of Adam and Eve alongside the Trees of Knowledge and Life. However, hidden in one of them is the serpent of temptation - again, indicating the choice: to eat the apple, or not to eat the apple?

The Lovers is the card of romantic choices, passion and temptation. The image shows two lovers who are close but, in the gap between them, is the snake of temptation. The face looking down represents the power of love, but it is linked with the Gemini star sign, so there are two ways to use this love - wisely or recklessly. As such, this is both an exciting and an intriguing card.

Although the symbolism of the two people who depict The Lovers implies that this card is about romantic relationships alone, it encompasses all relationships, but particularly close ones, and indeed the decisions that one makes around those relationships that impact one's life path.

This card refers to strong emotions, a choice of the heart that cannot be made by logic alone. Its divinatory meanings are love, beauty, harmony, perfection, trust, deep feelings, freedom of emotion, optimism, the necessity of trial, struggle between sacred and profane love, and a meaningful affair, perhaps one that already exists being enhanced in some way.

This card is not always about choice, but can be strongly about unity: the inner and outer paths - both expressions of the Divine must be brought together in unity. The Lovers show that our task is to recognise the underlying unity between these apparent opposites and to integrate them into our self. It illustrates the dangers and pitfalls that attend all choices, particularly those made in the name of love, and that affairs of the heart are neither easy nor straightforward.

Ultimately, the Lovers represent an outcome between past and present circumstances and the path ahead. It indicates there is currently, or will be, a relationship in your life which has forced you into experiencing some kind of trial or choice. If not about love, then it suggests a choice must be made that has heartfelt consequences. It offers temporary respite from existential loneliness. It is wise to move forward to the new opportunities awaiting you. The challenge first is to unify opposing forces within yourself to create a new, harmonious whole.

Geminis are recommended to carry one of these cards with them to illumine their paths, and to magnetise that for which they are asking. Go forth and claim the magic which is yours by using the symbolism of The Lovers as your guide!

★ THE MAGICIAN ★
Ruled by Mercury

Keywords ★ Initiative, Will, Independence

★ KEY THEMES ★

"Dancing in the Fire of Life"

Opportunity ★ Initiative ★ Interesting Prospects ★ Free Will ★ New Ventures ★ Intelligence ★ Apprenticeship ★ Potential Talents or Qualities Shining Through ★ Ability to Convince Others ★ Originality ★ Spontaneity ★ Flexibility ★ Possibilities ★ Skill ★ Adaptability ★ Duplicity ★ Free Spirit ★ Power ★ Influence ★ Cunning

Number ★ 1
Astrological Signs ★ Aries, Gemini & Virgo

THE STORY ★ The Magician is an effective, powerful man with a strong focus upon goals. He makes plans and then fulfils them. He is a skilled and clever character, who performs occult rituals, pouring energy from his extended hand which erupts into a pillar of living fire. As fire can transform what is added to it, this shaman can transform one thing into another: clay into brick, water into steam, fire into embers. While the Fool before him symbolises the unconscious, untainted mind, the Magician is the embodiment of conscious knowledge, with its ability to know and therefore manipulate the outside physical world. Like the Fool, the Magician wears a pointed hat, the apex of which alludes to the ability to draw down cosmic forces.

The image contains a Pentacle, Cup, Sword and Wand, as tokens of his mastery over the four elements. The Magician offers a choice of directions and the opportunity to take one of them; the Cup represents the realm of feeling and relationships; the Sword is connected with the mind and the logical, rational world; the Wand symbolises creativity and imagination; and the Pentacle is associated with the material, the body and the physical world. Opportunities are available in each, or all, of these areas. He represents vigour and talent in any chosen area, which are backed up by a strong urge or pull. Overall, the Magician represents desires made manifest on Earth through the power of thought. He is the mediator between the spiritual and the physical worlds, and with initiative and cunning, he decides which ideas will be made real.

THE LESSON ★ Generally, the Magician signifies fresh beginnings, the start of a new phase or cycle, and a directed sense of purpose. The Magician is a card of potential which points to the importance of a new enterprise. It's time to forget false modesty and to strike out in a new, dynamic, bold direction. Capitalise on your imaginative and creative skills. The fresh start the Magician implies should not be entered into lightly - there's often an element of trickery or doubt surrounding this card, however it is particularly auspicious for business ventures and financial matters because it shows that you have what it takes to succeed; indeed, all the necessary tools are at your disposal.

SYMBOLISM * ★ The Jungian archetype for the Magician is the Trickster, such as the Native American coyote. From the as-yet-untapped potential of the Fool, the Magician emerges as the determination to make things happen. This card therefore denotes confidence, decisiveness and an awareness of one's personal power and effect. You actually have the knowledge, skills and experience at hand but you must now concentrate on using these skills and also on marketing them. There is a suggestion that even if you don't feel confident, you should do your best to appear so, and you may need to use an element of trickery to achieve this - or to get what you want.

Its symbolism is youthful and dynamic, hinting at the vast creative forces being channelled through the body of the Magician with the help of the tools that are laid out before him, using these elements for the manifestation of his desires.

The Wand the Magician is pointing towards the sky symbolises his use of it to access Universal forces in order to amplify the power of his will and intentions.

The Magician's right hand, the symbol of action, points downwards to the four Tarot tools anchoring the energy. The inspiration gained through his spiritual connection with the Universal forces needs Earthly energy, so his body acts as a conduit for these ends.

In most cards he is represented as a travelling entertainer, a 'showman', part mountebank, part wiseman, and possibly also a trickster and illusionist. The Magician, in medieval Europe, lived on the fringes of the law and was regarded with a mixture of fascination and suspicion by the authorities and the people. He is always number One - at centre stage and in the spotlight. This apparent forthrightness can be misleading, for there is always something going on behind the scenes - sometimes even deception. The image exudes originality and confidence, which associates it with positive action, cleverness, cunning, individuality and creativity.

Traditionally the Magician was ruled by Aries, tying in with the fact that both Aries and the

Magician are number one in their respective astrological and Tarot sequences. As such, the Magician represents the ego, sitting like the Sun at the centre of the personality, with the Fire of will manifesting his desires into reality through the power of initiative.

The Magician's number is 1, the symbol of a new beginning, and the brim of his hat forms a number 8, the symbol of infinity and eternal life. He is depicted wearing a long robe and standing before a table, upon which lies a Cup, Wand, Sword and Pentacle, representing the four suits of the Minor Arcana, and the elements of Water, Fire, Air and Earth, which in turn stand for feeling, intuition, thought and sensation, the four functions of human consciousness. The four types of divination used that correspond with each element are (respectively): hydromancy, pyromancy, aeromancy, and geomancy. He holds a wand in his hand, and sometimes appears with a serpent coiled around his waist, combined to signify a person of authority with the power to do good. Surrounding him are greenery and flowers. He holds the wand towards the heavens, to symbolise the purity of his higher aspirations, while the other hand points downwards, towards Earth and matter.

The Magician is often dressed in white and red to represent spiritual purity and passion, demonstrating the essential duality of his nature. He is connected with the Greek Hermes, messenger of the Gods; he stands for the link between the gods and men, and this can also be perceived as the link between the conscious and the unconscious mind.

The Magician represents a child, an adolescent, a young boy or girl, a student, a person who is young at heart, open-minded, inquisitive, and dynamic; someone with a youthful temperament or demeanour, whatever their age; somebody who undertakes or achieves something new, or who is starting a period in their life where they can exert their free-spirited essence.

The alchemy of Fire is the Magician's great secret. His activating power changes one thing into another; he represents the toolmaker, the wand-pointer and the shaman. The Magician as shaman demonstrates the channelling of healing heat - the Fire of the Universe coming through the human being. Like any shaman, the Magician is a mediator between two worlds - the inner, spiritual plane and the outer, physical plane.

The Magician symbolises the complex nature of the world, of life and reality. He tells us that the Universe is a formidable cosmic game, and that reality is an illusion, a projection of our consciousness, and not to be trusted without question. He appears wise but he is also artful and cunning; his sideways glance puts us on our guard. In a spiritual context, the Magician shows that it is time to put intuition and psychic abilities to practical use. Indeed, this card stands for the availability of options in many areas, and offers the enthusiasm to follow hunches or one's inner directive. The Magician knows that creative achievement demands a certain diligence, self-discipline, craftiness and wiliness, and that if one wants to manifest something worthwhile, then they need to visualise the goal and work toward it without getting distracted. In the arts of healing and magic, intention is *everything*. 'What you see is what you get' is one way of putting it, so hold the end result in view and get to work. All ideas need a channel to bring them down to Earth, to make them real on the physical plane, otherwise they may fade away into the ethers, unrealised and unmanifested. Indeed, you must remember that the Magician works with both forms and the formless, and with the Magician on your side, you should be able to accomplish whatever you set out to achieve.

The Magician stands for a teacher-guide, a person who offers education and enlightenment to all pupils attending the first lesson in the School of Life. The energy embodied in the Magician is that of purpose, action, intention, potential, skill, craftiness, creativity and will. The Magician tells us that we all have the ability to get on with life, as long as we acknowledge and accept there are obstacles to be overcome. He also challenges us not to be deceived by the transient, material world, and to be aware that you are in a position to influence others now *and* in the long-term, but discretion is vital. Your originality and compassion are highlighted here, but beware of being too clever or manipulative.

When working alongside the Magician in your Tarot journey, ask yourself how you can begin to shift your focus in life from external things to your inner self, as by looking inward you can discover even greater treasures than the material world can offer. Its divinatory meanings are originality, individuality, positive action, creativity, self-reliance, imagination, self-confidence, spontaneity, ingenuity, flexibility, self-control, deception and mastery. Generally, he signifies new beginnings, the start of a fresh cycle, a sense of purpose, willpower and initiative. The Magician is a card of potential, showing the importance of a new enterprise. The Magician is ultimately imparting the message that a great reserve of power and energy is available, and it is up to the seeker (you) how it will be used. Powerfully, he shows us that life is a magical act, and our mind the magician. Further, the Magician might well be ageless, just like Gemini itself. Go forth and make your claim!

★ THE FOOL ★
Ruled by Uranus & the Element of Air

Keywords ★ Beginnings, Innocence, Exploration

★ KEY THEMES ★

"Trusting Your Inner Elf"

Fresh Beginnings ★ Adventure ★ Quest ★ Excitement ★ Asserting Your Independence ★ Creative Solutions ★ Spontaneity ★ Egolessness ★ Innocence ★ The Need For Optimism ★ Naiveté ★ Unexpected Opportunities ★ Courage ★ Folly ★ Happy-Go-Lucky Mortal, About to Step Off a Cliff into the Abyss ★ Impulse

Meditation ★ "I have the courage to step forward; I am not afraid of the unknown."

Number ★ Zero (or 22 in some decks)

Astrological Signs ★ Aquarius, Gemini, Libra & Aries

THE STORY ★ The Fool card symbolises the state of potential from which all possibilities arise. It is the purest embodiment of the self on the quest for spiritual awakening. When the Fool appears in a Tarot spread, it suggests that you are about to embark on a journey that will fundamentally change you - either literally or by changing your outlook on life. You may not be certain of what lies ahead, but you must be willing to take the chance.

The Fool is a foolish man. And as such, he knows everything, but is unaware that he does. Or, he possesses all the gifts, all the truths, all the wisdom, all the joys, all the wonders of the seen and unseen worlds, but is totally unaware of it. He must therefore submit himself to the various trials of life to develop his faculties and become an enlightened being. The Fool represents the Self on a journey, who grows and learns with each new encounter. Wide-eyed and innocent as a newborn child, The Fool has descended from the celestial realms, eager to begin his mystical journey on the path towards enlightenment. All is new to him and he has not yet learned to fear. Living from moment to moment, going forward without plan nor care, unaware of potential perils and joyful, in his luggage he carries the memories, instincts and experiences of past lives, waiting to be utilised this time around. He carries a wand symbolising the pure faith of his actions, upon which sits a head that looks backwards, representing The Fool's past as he moves ever-forward. The dog leaping and bounding behind him symbolises the purity of the animal nature of our physical bodies and is seen in playful harmony with The Fool. The backdrop is suffused with green, the colour of growth, and the sky is filled with the fresh light of a spring season, signalling shining, new life. Like the court jesters who maintained his tradition, The Fool is truthful, and has no contaminating malice or desires.

SYMBOLISM *★ This card depicts the Fool wandering off, his few possessions slung over his shoulder in a small bag hung from a pilgrim's staff, oblivious to the chasm ahead, with his dog jumping at his leg. Symbolically, his bag carries his experiences. He does not abandon them, for he is not thoughtless, they simply do not control him in the way that *our* traumas or memories so often control our lives. The stick upon which his bag casually hangs, is, in some interpretations, actually a wand, a symbol of power and magic. The Fool card's image symbolises the instinctive life force that both holds him back and urges him on. Like its ruler Uranus, the Fool is the spirit of chaos, of the unexpected, but also about innocence and the simple joys of living. This card belongs anywhere in the deck, in combination with and between any of the other cards, offering an animating force to more static images and symbols. As such, he assists during times of transition, and also in times of difficult passage.

The Fool's staff represents the Suit of Wands, symbolic of passionate, fiery energy. He grasps the staff firmly, as he does all of life's opportunities, and although it is a symbol of power, the Fool uses it in a playful manner.

The Fool's cloak is usually blue, representing his inner search for wisdom and truth. And when he finds his enlightenment, he will be eager to communicate it to others.

The Fool is usually the first card in the Tarot deck, the starting point of the Tarot 'experience'. In some early decks he appeared at the end of the Major Arcana rather than at the beginning, as he not only begins our journey but may also accompany us throughout it - this is essentially because he symbolises our very self. When he first sets out at the beginning of his path, he is a stranger to his inner self and lives primarily in his conscious mind, but by the end of his journey he has glimpsed the deeper mysteries of his real self. The Fool seeks the truth, and turns his attention towards the spirit in search of it. There is in the Fool an element of the Divine trickster, and even though the Fool doesn't know what he is doing in the sense of logical thought, he moves from an impulse that arises out of the infinite possibilities emanating from the state represented by the number 'zero'. The Fool is simple, innocent, trusting and ignorant of the potential trials, setbacks and pitfalls that await him, and he is prepared to abandon his old ways and follow his quest by taking a leap into the unknown. Indeed, the Fool represents the need to let go of old ways and begin something new, untested and unexperienced. For those willing to follow the Fool's example and deviate from the path society has set out for us, this leap can bring joy, adventure, and finally, for those with the courage to continue even when the path becomes fearsome, the leap will bring peace, knowledge and liberation.

Containing all possibilities, the Fool represents the phenomenon of synchronicity or coincidences between happenings, and is the part of us that unconsciously connects to the greater Universal whole, so things are constantly happening to us that involve the unspoken and often unacknowledged links between our thoughts and the events outside of ourselves. If you are open to magic, you will accept these synchronicities on an intellectual level, and in turn will notice such events more frequently and learn to appreciate them more fully.

This card can be said to represent the human soul that is unselfconsciously happy to be alive, that does not yet reflect back upon itself, the spark of life that reincarnates again and again until it truly awakens to itself. Reincarnation is the secret key to the Fool, and the Fool is indeed the 'secret' key, or at least significantly the first door which opens us up to the rest of the Tarot experience. The Fool, whose awareness is limited to the present moment, moves from moment to moment, life to life, without intellectual consideration or care for what has gone before and what will be in the future. Representing innocence, the Fool is perpetually young and always starting afresh. He believes in himself and instinctively trusts his body and the general flow of life.

Astrologically, the Fool is ruled by the Air element, making it as free as the wind. Uranus, considered the most eccentric of the planets, gives the card's symbolism qualities of intellectual brilliance, intuitive flashes, lawlessness, reform, inventiveness and originality. Linked to this rebellious planet, it also promises mystery, a dash of genius, adventure, and a great opportunity to reinvent your life. It impels you to listen to your own inner guidance about following your dreams while still staying open to outside guidance and information; actively seek any insight you may need for your leap.

Although some divinatory meanings of this card are thoughtlessness, insecurity, folly, apathy, frivolity, extravagance, lack of discipline, immaturity, irrationality, hesitation, indecision, delirium, frenzy, enthusiasm and naivety, it also proclaims that nothing can harm you, whatever you do, so take a risk! It does, however, advise to look before you leap - a measured, calculated risk will reap the greatest rewards - and lessons. This card symbolises new beginnings in all senses, courageous leaps into some new phase of life, and is a particularly potent symbol when that jump is taken from some inner prompting and deep feeling rather than careful planning.

Not limited by ordinary social conventions and uncomplicated and unanalytical by nature, the Fool is never afraid to believe in something Divine or greater than ego. Naturally flowing, trusting, naïve and spontaneous, the Fool often plunges into the cosmic experience without fear or expectation. And indeed, it is the Fool in each of us which urges us away from lethargy and towards enlightenment and transformation without fear of the future. And along your travels, it is also worth noting and reminding yourself that even a fool can have flashes of great wisdom and sudden lightning bolt thoughts, reminiscent of the brilliant but ever-unpredictable Uranus, ruler of your fellow Air sign Aquarius.

* Please note that the images described are not found in all Tarot decks. The images in different decks can differ considerably.

THE TAROT'S SUIT OF SWORDS ★ REPRESENTING THE AIR ELEMENT

The Swords correspond with the Air element and are an especially interesting and meaningful metaphor. Swords, or the mind, organise by dividing, and quite literally cutting through things. Being of the Air element, the Swords are associated with ideas, the intellect, mental activity, thought processes, and mental insights, attitudes and clarity. Air cannot be seen, gripped, grasped or commanded of, and can only be felt with subtle 'other' senses - the higher mind being one of them. We know the air is there through its apparent physical presence such as wisps of wind, but we cannot see it, touch it or even embrace it. In this way, the Swords suit can signify a certain elusiveness, something that can somehow evade us. But it is nonetheless a powerful force. With the Air suit, illusions are recognised and shattered in the pursuit of the inner kernel of truth, knowledge and wisdom that the Swords embody - but the quest is fraught with painful lessons and is not always easy. These challenges will lead to greater understanding. The story of Swords begins with the core connection to the all-wise, all-seeing eye of the spirit.

This Divine essence first manifests itself in the mind and then those thoughts create form. Everything you see results from an initial thought that was put into action. As well as relating to the conscious direction of the intellect and will, the Swords also reveal hidden motivations and attitudes that can influence a situation.

Cards from this suit advise us to either go to the core of the problem or to cut ourselves free in order to start afresh. Considered to be powerful and potentially destructive and dangerous, the Tarot Swords can indicate battles and enemies, but they can also be used constructively, to summon courage and a more conscious and astute quality of mind. Even though they have long had a reputation as harbingers of unhappiness and discomfort, this suit still serves a useful purpose. Without the ability to use reason and logic we risk being constantly swept away by our emotions, with all the potential for disaster that this could bring. The Swords can therefore assist in bringing about increased clarity and foresight, which we can use to avert trouble that may be brewing, and nip explosiveness in the bud. The Swords may be connected with hostility, sorrows, loss, struggle, action, change, bitterness, power, oppression, malice and conflict, but they are also associated with fortitude, decisiveness, audacity, tact, fairness, strength, bravery, ambition, force and truth, as well as with ideas and communication. Swords are almost always double-edged, which symbolises the fine balance that is needed between the intellect and power, and how these two forces can be used for good or evil. Overall, the Suit of Swords reveals our state of mind and how we use its mighty force. In a deck of playing cards, Swords correspond to Spades.

THE LUCKY 13 ★ GEMINIAN TIPS FOR INCREASED MAGIC, LUCK & MAGNETISM

1 ★ Incorporate Geminian symbols into your daily life to remind yourself of your soul's mission.

2 ★ Use the crystal Agate in any form in your daily life - wear it, meditate with it, hold it and carry it with you everywhere! Agate tunes and strengthens the body and mind and imparts a sense of strength and courage. Its power comes from its ability to promote circulation of energy around the body. Agates come in a vast array of colours and patterns, but all agates are protective and nurture natural talents and relationships, acting as shields to protect you on your spiritual journey. Grounding yet energetic, agate is a powerful healer, encouraging emotions or states of being that assist in attracting wonderful things to you.

3 ★ Wear or surround yourself with the colours yellow, silver and jade green.

4 ★ Learn the way of the Archer by learning to engage in deeper thought, greater spiritual awareness and broader vision. Sagittarius has much to teach the Geminian soul. Allow your mind to soar to greater heights … Take a course in or read a book on philosophy … Widen your horizons, mentally and physically … Engage in international travel, meet foreign people … Throw an extravagant dinner party and instigate deep and meaningful conversations …

Ask everyone you meet what the meaning of life is ... Cultivate wisdom ... Enrol in higher education - no matter your age! ... Attend cultural festivals and events ... Study a religious or spiritual way of life ... Talk less about people and more about ideas ... Gaze at the stars and feel the awe at the unimaginable depth and dimensions of the Universe ... it's *all* within you!

5 ★ Use your lucky numbers 3 and 5, whenever you are needing an extra stroke of luck.

6 ★ Magnify and celebrate your agile mind, your flexibility, your youthful exuberance and your childlike wonder and curiosity.

7 ★ Remind yourself of your mission constantly, that is by speaking, breathing and *truly living* your dreams and insights - try to see any goals or projects that are important to you through to the end!

8 ★ Focus your energies on expanding your brilliant intellect, and transforming yourself through your higher mind - which are strongly accessible to the clever, intelligent and peppy Geminian psyche. Connect with your powerful brainpower and inborn love of gathering information and knowledge through any means possible. Knock yourself out!

9 ★ Use your innate powers of sociability, your gift of the gab and your natural charm to draw that which you desire towards you. If you can develop simple faith in the positive outcome of events, you can easily use your inborn charisma and mind power to great creative effect.

10 ★ Tap into and utilise your ability to connect, link, gather, disseminate and disperse information and transform others through communicating your inspiring and uplifting thoughts and ideas. But to do that, you'll need to concentrate and focus on just *one* important thing at a time! Even though you are a terrific jack-of-all-trades multi-tasker, directing your energies in one direction at a time will work wonders.

11 ★ View your restless nature as a strength and call forth the powers of your entertaining, fun-loving, humorous, gifted, unique self. Be who you *really* are, without reservation or apology, and the rest will fall into place.

12 ★ Become the 'Light-hearted Enlightener' of others - and yourself - that you were born to be! The world needs cheekier, mischievous, audacious elves!

13 ★ Once you have mastered purer focus and direction upon one or two special projects, goals or dreams, learn to share the resulting abundance, insights and knowledge with others so they too can walk the Higher Path!

HAVE YOU PACKED YOUR MAGICAL BAG FOR THE JOURNEY?

If you wish to increase and draw more luck, love and abundance into your life, a power pack is essential. For Geminians, I would recommend carrying or wearing the following items on you on your travels. Then just sit back and watch as magic pours into your experiences and realities, both inner and outer!

★ One of each of the following gemstones: Alexandrite, Agate, Citrine, Emerald
★ Tarot Cards; The Lovers and The Magician (and The Fool card too, if you wish)
★ A deer in any form (use your imagination!)
★ Something made of silver
★ A caduceus symbol in any form
★ A postcard or image from a tropical place (representing your Sanguine disposition). Bon Voyage!
★ A postcard from the future to yourself, proclaiming, 'Wish You Were Here!'

A FINAL WORD ⋆ TAPPING INTO THE MAGIC OF GEMINI

There is something inherently magical about Gemini the Twins. Blessed with a wonderful intellect, a vivacious manner, a brilliant mind and a bedazzling wit, you truly are the enlivening social entertainer of the zodiac, affecting everyone around you with your abundance of youthful vitality. Flexible and nimble, you love to roam, wander, hop, jump and skip, leaving a trail of invisible glitter wherever you go! A refreshing breath of fresh Air, you are the Peter Pan of the zodiacal experience, possessing an enviable sense of wonder, adventure and buoyant hope.

Inside anyone who has a strong Gemini influence in their natal chart is a person who longs to find their true soul mate, the mysterious 'other' twin who will make you feel complete. Communication is a lifeline to you, and few would ever realise that an outwardly confident Gemini is often feeling desperately alone and lost. There is also a deep sense, albeit subconscious, that the search for the lost 'other' will never come to fruition. The Gemini soul is a lot more complex than its characteristic surface superficiality suggests. But nothing is dull or forgettable about the sparkling Twins. The cosmos has endowed you with the precious and wondrous gifts of sociability, intelligence, spirit, a good sense of humour, the ability to find and create fun, and of course that characteristic twinkle in your eye. Whether you are fully cognisant of it or not, a magical reservoir of energy is available to you to tap into whenever it is needed.

Finally, to attune yourself to luck, harmony and success, Geminians should wear, eat, inhale, meditate upon, create, design, and dance with any or all of the suggested luck-enhancers for your Sun sign to receive the most beneficial astral vibrations these 'boosters' can offer you. Wearing, decorating and working with the amazing powers of all your lucky guides, animals, crystals, colours, woods, cards, herbs, foods, places, talismans, planetary influences, charms, numbers, and other magical tips contained within the words of this very book, will bring you greater abundance, love, magic, energy, happiness and personal power, and attract all manner of things to you like bees to sweet flowers. This, my Geminian friends, I promise you - and Aquarians *never* lie.

Good luck on the rest of your amazing life journey, and may LUCK always smile upon you!

Lani is also available for personal Astrology, Numerology, Aura * & Tarot reading consultations, via post, email, Skype and in-person.

Please email lalana76@bigpond.com
For more information.

In-person only

Facebook Page ★ Astrology Magic

Other Books in the **Lucky Astrology** Series

Lucky Astrology ★ Aries
Lucky Astrology ★ Taurus
Lucky Astrology ★ Cancer
Lucky Astrology ★ Leo
Lucky Astrology★ Virgo
Lucky Astrology ★ Libra
Lucky Astrology ★ Scorpio
Lucky Astrology ★ Sagittarius
Lucky Astrology ★ Capricorn
Lucky Astrology ★ Aquarius
Lucky Astrology ★ Pisces

Order your copies now, from White Light Publishing House, at www.whitelightpublishingau.com

www.ingramcontent.com/pod-product-compliance
Lightning Source LLC
Chambersburg PA
CBHW052129010526
44113CB00034B/1210